P9-DEW-400

LIVING FINANCIALLY FREE

James L. Paris

HARVEST HOUSE PUBLISHERS
Eugene, OR 97402

Except where otherwise indicated, all Scripture quotations in this book are taken from the New American Standard Bible, ©1960, 1962, 1963, 1968, 1971, 1972, 1973, 1975, 1977 by The Lockman Foundation. Used by permission.

LIVING FINANCIALLY FREE

Copyright ©1995 by Harvest House Publishers
Eugene, Oregon 97402

ISBN 1-56507-331-2

All rights reserved. No portion of this book may be reproduced in any form without the written permission of the Publisher.

Printed in the United States of America.

ACKNOWLEDGMENTS

I would like to give special thanks to Bob Yetman, who worked tirelessly for several weeks in helping me complete this project. Without him this book would never have been a reality. My wife and our children, Jim and Joy, allowed me to work on this book during the past several months, which was a sacrifice for our family. I would also like to thank my staff and the following people for their part in making this book possible: Deannie Benge, Raymond Pena, Carmen Paris, Lynn Brown, Jack Webb, Gail Full, Pam Wray, Scott Thevenet, and Jean Sample.

I also thank my editors, Steve Miller and Ray Oehm, as well as the Harvest House staff, for their dedication to this project.

This book is dedicated to the memory of Betty Paris, my grandmother. In 1992 I visited her in the hospital. Although she was critically ill, she told me she was not going to die there and that she would get better so we could write a book together—a book that would help people save money. She put up a tough fight but never made it out of the hospital. Those were the last words she said to me, and though she did not help write the book, she very much inspired it.

FOREWORD

As the host of a national talk show I have welcomed many good financial counselors and experts to my microphone. But several years ago I encountered a man who was special.

Why special?

Because he combined a grasp of clear principles and biblical principles with an uncommon soundness of nitty-gritty practical advice. This man took biblical principles and put shoe leather to them. At the same time he avoided many of the fads and fancies of Christian financial counselors who, while often well-meaning (and often not), have thrown themselves and their counselees over the cliffs of speculation, panic-mongering, and legalism.

But not this man.

I listened to him counsel hurting people with gracious insight and surefooted guidance. I heard him give wisdom to others who wanted to avoid mistakes and maximize their material wealth for godly purposes.

That guest, of course, was Jim Paris. Later, when I began listening to his own talk show, *The Christian Consumer Advocate,* I heard him help caller after caller scramble out of the surf of financial despair onto the solid rock of hope. And I heard him help those who wanted to get ahead as they scaled the foothills and even the mountains of achievement.

In other words, I have confidence in Jim Paris.

And I have confidence in Jim Paris' urgently needed book, *Living Financially Free.*

Why do I say "urgently needed"?

Just look around. Although the Bible has more to say on wealth than on almost any other subject, if you take the sheer mass of passages, it seems that the church has more misconceptions about wealth than on almost any other subject, if you take the sheer mass of wreckage. Positive confessionism? It's in its heyday. Rampant "sell-the-house, hock-the-retirement, head-for-the-hills" doom-and-gloomism? It's selling books like hotcakes.

Financial heresy would be hilarious if it weren't for the lives it is ruining.

Yes, Christians are facing a financial crisis, largely one of our own making. But if we took the time to look into the sober-minded, commonsense advice of the Scriptures, then applied that advice in a practical way, we would find that spirituality and practicality combine for the most dynamic contentment and fulfillment possible.

And this is what Jim Paris helps you achieve with this book. There is virtually no subject uncovered, no controversy left untackled. The benefits of the advice stored in this treasury far outweigh the price you will pay to purchase it.

Finally, let me say that my ultimate endorsement is that I have not only seen others prosper from the guidance found in these pages, but it has helped me as well. *Living Financially Free* is a reliable guide for these confusing times for Christians who are searching for all they should be for themselves, for their families, and for God. I commend it to you. I know you will be excited about the change it can bring in your life.

—MARLIN MADDOUX

CONTENTS

AN INVITATION TO
FINANCIAL FREEDOM

I had a very harsh introduction into church financial training. One Sunday morning my wife and I were in a large denominational church in Orlando, Florida—a church we had been attending for about a year. Inside the bulletin was an announcement about the church's need for financial counselors. My wife nudged me and pointed out this ministry opportunity. I had been struggling personally for some time trying to find a way to serve the Lord in ministry, and this sounded inviting.

Several days later I joined the training program to become a financial counselor for my church. At the time I was a stockbroker for a large brokerage firm and felt that my financial skills were more than adequate to teach people about budgeting and getting out of debt. The counseling program was advertised as a sort of last stop before bankruptcy. In fact, many of the people who were receiving counseling had already gone through bankruptcy.

My first day was quite interesting, to say the least! I expected the class to be compiled of CPAs and financial planners, but this was not the case. Everyone in the class but I was female, and not only were they not financial professionals, but they were all stay-at-home moms. (Like my wife, they chose more difficult careers than financial planning!)

It was clear that the only two seasoned financial people in the room were myself and the instructor, who happened to be a CPA. I naively thought that my background in finances would be an asset to this counseling program, but I was wrong. I learned very quickly that I was not welcome, as the instructor kept me after the first class to lecture me privately about not using the counseling program as a way to procure clients. From my point of view this was the most ridiculous thing I had ever heard, since how could clients be gained for a stockbroker out of a program that counsels the close-to-bankruptcy and the outright bankrupt? I stuck with the class for several weeks after that initial meeting, but as each week progressed I began to feel more and more unwelcome. Finally I realized it was time to leave the class.

Recently I was asked to speak at a church in northern Florida in both the morning and evening services. I was planning to teach about credit cards, life insurance, etc. After the morning service, the pastor pleaded with me not to talk about life insurance in the evening service because a member of his church was a life insurance agent and threatened to stand up and interrupt the service if anything was said that he didn't fully agree with.

I acquiesced and said nothing about life insurance. But I was appalled that during my entire presentation that evening, despite the fact that I gracefully tried to avoid confrontation by not speaking on life insurance, this insurance agent was vehemently shaking his head and speaking to people around him as he obviously disagreed with everything I said for the full two hours.

Money is a strange thing, and it gets even stranger within the walls of a church. Maybe this is true because it is something we all have in common: We all possess money. It is certainly something we all have opinions about. These opinons may get in the way of the real facts, the hard truth about money that we all need to hear but few of us are willing to listen to. I hope that someday our churches in America can become more mature about their approach to financial education.

No one has all the answers, and thus a variety of ideas should be welcomed and taught. Financial education should not be viewed as a turf battle; the church should find a way to use qualified and experienced financial professionals and a wide variety of resource material to teach Christians how to make the most of the money God has blessed them with.

This book is more than an author's attempt to assemble a few ideas; it is really a compilation of my life experiences in dealing with people from all walks of life and from every financial perspective imaginable. I am most impacted by the lessons I have learned from watching the true-life stories of both good and bad stewards of God's money. My wish for you is simple: financial freedom. I hope this book provides you with a foundation to build on in order to receive the highest reward of all: "Well done, good and faithful servant."

THE FREEDOM PRINCIPLES

You will find this book filled with Freedom Principles. These truths about money are really a collection of useful nuggets of financial information that for the most part are a product of my radio broadcast. If a host is to solve a caller's financial dilemma within two to three minutes during a radio broadcast, he must provide solid financial advice in a short window of time, and so the Freedom Principles were born. These Principles are consumer strategies that have worked for thousands of listeners of my national radio broadcast and they will work for you too.

This first chapter contains the most important of these Principles as we lay down the biblical foundation that will lead us along the path to financial freedom. These overarching Principles must play an integral role in every element of our financial life.

FREEDOM PRINCIPLE
Money is not inherently evil.

One way some Christians have chosen to deal with money is to simply categorize it as evil and thus something not to be concerned about. This belief lends itself to the philosophy that "to be poor is to be godly." People living by this credo don't have to be wise spenders of their money, since success (amassing money) would be a sin anyway. One man who was obviously a follower of this philosophy told me that if he were offered two jobs with the same reponsibilities, all things being equal, he would take the lower-paying job because in his words, "It would keep him humble." This kind of thinking is without scriptural foundation. It baffles me how we can read Scripture and the stories of the people who were wealthy and used by God and still somehow adopt this "poverty theology." Some of the great biblical characters who were described as wealthy include Abraham, David, Solomon, and Job. In no way did their material wealth interfere with their ability to serve God.

FREEDOM PRINCIPLE
**How much money you have is far less
important than how you manage it.**

The parable of the talents (Matthew 25:14–30) teaches us that we are to be good stewards no matter how much or little money God has blessed us with. In this parable Jesus describes three servants who were given one, two, and five units of money respectively. Though the three servants had responsibility for different amounts of money, they all were called to be good stewards.

I believe there is a certain significance in each of the three servants being given a different amount of money. They appear to represent, in essence, a lower class, a middle class, and an upper class. It is also intriguing to note that the servant with the least amount of money did the least (verse 25): He buried the talent in the ground.

FREEDOM PRINCIPLE
What we own is not ours.

Each of the persons in the parable of the talents is referred to as a servant. What does a servant or a slave own? Nothing. His possessions belong to his master, not to him. This is really what stewardship is all about: recognizing that as Christians everything belongs to Christ. Our role becomes one of a steward. A steward is one who manages something on behalf of the real owner, who will eventually ask for an accounting.

FREEDOM PRINCIPLE
We are all called to be good stewards, regardless of how much money we are entrusted with.

The parable provides no excuse for the servant with the one talent. Many people today rely on the excuse, "If I only had more, I would be a better steward." Stewardship comes into play in virtually every financial circumstance that we as Christians are in. The truth is that if you are a poor money manager right now you will do just as poorly if you have ten times what you possess now.

An old Chinese proverb says, "If all the money in the world were divided equally among everyone, we would all be right back where we are now in 30 days." It is strange to hear the stories of multimillionaires who count every penny and some who even wear ten-year-old suits. The truth is simple: They are rich because of how careful they are with their money. Their good stewardship will not allow them to spend frivously even if they could justify it by the fact that they may now "have money to burn."

FREEDOM PRINCIPLE
There are penalties for poor stewardship.

God's laws are designed to protect us, not deny us from pleasure. Many people have learned by experience that violating God's laws creates a natural consequence. This applies to economics as well.

We read in the parable of the talents that the servant who buried his talent in the ground had the money taken away from him. The master gave it to the servant who had doubled his five talents to become ten. It makes good economic sense, then, to be wise stewards of what God has given us. Careless stewardship produces fruitless results—always.

FREEDOM PRINCIPLE
There are rewards for good stewardship.

According to the parable of the talents, those who are careless managers of their possessions will lose them, but those who are wise managers will gain more. Two of the servants doubled their money; the one who doubled his amount to ten talents was given the talent that had been entrusted to the slothful servant.

This represents both direct rewards from good stewardship and God's additional blessing (the additional talent given).

What is especially noteworthy about this parable is that nowhere do we see Jesus praise or criticize people on the basis of how much money they have. Rather, people are rewarded according to the way they *manage* their money.

FREEDOM PRINCIPLE
Christians can use debt wisely.

Debt is a controversial issue, with quite a few variations in opinons within Christian circles. Most often, even those who believe Christians should not have debt make exceptions to their beliefs for larger purchases such as houses and cars. That brings me to ask this question: "How can a true biblical principle be inconsistently applied to only those situations that we want it to?" I have read articles and chapters in books discussing the so-called strong theological basis for Christians never having any debt of any kind, yet later read in those very same texts that there are "exceptions" to these principles.

As with most matters of controversy, the truth can usually be found somewhere in the middle, and this case is no different. We find many warnings about the danger of debt in Scripture, but I do not believe there is any such verse placing an absolute restriction on Christians having debt. Many theologians have done studies looking for a final answer to this long-debated question, but none have legitimately found a biblical case for the absolute prohibition of the use of debt. This does not mean that we as Christians have a license to go into an unlimited amount of debt for any reason at any time, but rather that the wise use of debt is possible, and that in many cases it is the only way most people can invest in a home of their own or purchase reliable automobiles.

WHAT THE BIBLE SAYS ABOUT DEBT

1. **We are to repay what we borrow:** "*The wicked borrows and does not pay back*" (Psalm 37:21). We should take seriously the fact that any money we borrow must be paid back as promised.
2. **Debt can create financial bondage:** "*The borrower becomes the lender's slave*" (Proverbs 22:7). Although we find no absolute prohibition of debt in Scriptures, we also find no encouragement for us to get into debt. In fact, most of the scriptural mentions of debt are warnings about the dangers of misusing debt.

As I mentioned earlier, some people teach that Christians should have no debt at all. They usually base their argument on Romans 13:8, "Owe nothing to anyone." Interestingly, however, after they make their case that the Bible prohibits debt, they still somehow allow for exceptions in the case of homes and other large purchases.

A more thorough reading of Romans 13 in its entirety gives us a better understanding of what is being taught, which is simply that *we should repay our debts as they become due.* The concept of repayment of debt, which is simply an element of Christian integrity, is supported in Scripture (e.g. Psalm 37:21). There is no one biblical command that places an absolute prohibition on Christians from having debt. But of course our use of debt must fall under the same stewardship commitment that should be evident in all other aspects of our financial lives. The use of credit involves great discernment and wisdom, and I will address those issues in Chapter 4.

FREEDOM PRINCIPLE
**Invest to make money, not
political statements.**

Without question, Christians should not ignore their moral and spiritual convictions in the business world. We must, however, approach these issues with a sense of logic and practicality.

Generally, I am not a supporter of the socially responsible investing movement. While I do not agree with many policies and positions of corporate America, my refusal to invest in these companies does not adversely affect them in any meaningful way. There is one exception: if a company is issuing new stock. In the case of a new offering, I am in fact providing operating capital to the company making the stock offering. But most people do not buy stock this way. For example, if I buy 100 shares of Disney or IBM, I am not giving these companies my money, nor am I financially helping them, because my money goes to another investor like me.

The problem becomes more complex when you consider that a stock mutual fund may be investing in more than 100 different stocks. Investors who follow the approach of socially responsible investing may find it a literal nightmare to examine all of the corporate policies of all the companies in a mutual fund portfolio. Additionally, some funds turn over more than 50% of the stocks in their portfolio each year!

The solution, many would say, is socially responsible mutual funds. A recent such fund, The Timothy Plan, is now being marketed to the Christian community as the investment of choice for those who want to punish corporate America for their godless ways. The fund has retained the services of the American Family Association to determine which stocks do not espouse Christian values so they can avoid purchasing these shares in their fund. While this fund is without question the most overtly Christian, it is not the only socially responsible mutual fund. Listed below are several others, ranging from funds that stay away from environmentally insensitive companies to those that avoid companies that manufacture birth control pills, tobacco, or firearms.

SOCIALLY RESPONSIBLE MUTUAL FUNDS

Calvert Group	800-368-2748
Covenant Fund	800-652-4352
Domini Social Equity Fund	800-762-6814
Dreyfus Third Century Fund	800-645-6561
Green Century Fund	800-934-7336
New Alternatives	516-466-0808

Pax World Fund	800-767-1729
Pioneer Funds	800-225-6292
Progressive Environmental	800-367-7814
Rightime Social Awareness	800-242-1421
Timothy Plan	800-846-7526
Women's Equity Fund	800-424-2295

When people ask me which socially responsible mutual funds they should invest in, I tell them to invest in the ones that are consistently making money for their investors (which limits the possibilities significantly). To make my point, I use General Electric as an example many times on my radio show. If I'm watching the "Tonight Show" and Jay Leno tells a tasteless, off-color joke, should I sell all of my mutual funds that invest in GE since GE owns NBC? Or should I sell all stocks of corporations that advertise on liberal TV programs like "Phil Donahue"?

While some funds in the socially responsible category have had good performance, almost all lag the overall return of the market. This is not surprising when you realize that these money managers spend so much of their energy deciding what *not* to buy rather than what to buy.

If you really want to hit a company and hurt its pocketbook, *don't buy its products*. Donald Wildman of the American Family Association has literally brought corporations to their knees by launching national boycotts of their products and services. In this way, you are truly depriving these firms of revenue.

For further reading on the topic, Gary Moore has written *The Thoughful Christian's Guide to Investing* (Zondervan, 1991). Gary is a professional stockbrocker and is very much a proponent of socially responsible investing, although I don't agree with his approach, his book covers the subject well.

My opinion is simple: If these funds perform, invest in them. If they don't, stay away from them. Investing should be to make money, not political statements. In any case, I would not invest in them if they do not have at least a three-year above-average track record.

This chapter is intended as a foundation upon which we can build throughout the rest of the book. As you continue reading, keep this in mind: Money does not come with its own instruction manual. We as Christians should recognize that the Bible is that manual.

Even as the rich young ruler had to make a decision between his possessions and following the Lord, we too must make that decision today. The song puts it well: "Jesus, be Lord of all. . . . If He's not Lord of everything, He's not Lord at all." As we now begin our journey, which ends in financial freedom, I encourage you to recognize the lordship of Christ over your finances, and the fact that He is the true key to achieving financial freedom.

2

BEYOND GLOOM
AND DOOM

One afternoon while I was working in my office, one of my assistants asked if he could transfer a call to me. He explained briefly that there were two people on the phone who were emotionally distraught about some financial decisions they had made recently.

Of course I took the call, and a couple in their mid-fifties explained to me how they had recently read a book about a coming financial collapse. Part of the advice in the book was a recommendation to the reader to liquidate all retirement plans to be able to pay off mortgage debt. This couple had followed that advice, but they became very emotionally upset when they visited their accountant, who was preparing their tax return for that year, and he explained to them the consequences of liquidating their retirement plans.

What they had not realized was that because they were younger than 59½ years of age, they would be subject to an IRS penalty of 10% on all the money they had withdrawn. Furthermore, they now had to pay taxes on all of these funds for the current tax year, which moved them to a higher tax bracket. This couple, who had saved their entire life to be able to enjoy their retirement, now realized that they had lost about 50% of their retirement nest egg because of the bad advice they received through the book.

Unfortunately, the action they took was irreversible, so there was nothing I could do to help them. They realized too late that they had fallen prey to the kind of advice which so frequently comes from "gloom-and-doom" authors. I hope this chapter serves as a warning and perhaps as a rebuttal to the popular message that we should all build financial bomb shelters because the end of the world is coming.

FREEDOM PRINCIPLE
Be cautious about following the advice of "gloom-and-doom" gurus.

IS A COLLAPSE ON THE WAY?

The question of a coming economic collapse has embedded in it a substantial number of peripheral issues, none of which is easy to tackle. The truth is that no one really knows how to accurately predict the future of the economy, much less any coming collapse. I hope that cooler heads will prevail as this issue becomes more and more discussed by certain authors and speakers. This chapter will not only unfold the issue but also give you a detailed picture of the danger inherent in accepting the gloom-and-doom philosophies of the day.

I should point out that various degrees of gloom and doom are being espoused today. While it is easy to disagree with the most extreme thinkers on the subject, some of the more responsible conservative writers and thinkers on the topic have rendered a great service to all of us by pointing out there is a large national debt and that as financial weathermen they see a dark cloud on the horizon. The most outrageous advisers discredit themselves with their "Chicken Little" predictions that time and time again fail to come true. We should, however, be willing to listen to the more reasonable voices of concern.

My advice centers mostly on how to react to the possibility of these events. In fairness, I want to state that I have no greater ability to predict the future of this country's economics than anyone else. I am not saying that there will never be an economic collapse, nor would I predict whether there will be one. I am simply trying to help you get ready financially for *any* economic challenge that may be on the horizon.

Now let's look at some of the specific tactics that the gloom-and-doom advisers are using today.

1. They make predictions, but deny they are doing so.
2. They create a win-win scenario by creating such a loose set of predictions that they can always claim they were right regardless of the outcome.
3. They give potentially destructive financial advice, but deny that people following their advice will be adversely affected if their predictions are wrong.
4. They know their predictions of doom will sell books and newsletters (and, in many cases, investments that they will make a commission on).

FINANCIAL COLLAPSES AND BIBLE PROPHECY

FREEDOM PRINCIPLE
**Do not confuse prophecy of end-time
events with your investment strategy.**

Christians have always been predisposed to believe in apocalyptic predictions. In the case of the possibility of an economic collapse, many of us are waiting anxiously to accept as fact any and all gloom-and-doom predictions. This is true because, from a Christian perspective, any governmental or economic collapse brings with it the hope that the second coming may take place soon. In one sense this is a healthy perspective to have, since even Jesus Himself said we are to "be on the alert, for you do not know which day your Lord is coming" (Matthew 24:42).

However, we should never build all our financial plans and strategies around predictions that the actual end is upon us. History abounds with well-meaning predictions that were never fulfilled. For example, when I was a student at Central Bible College, I found an interesting older book about the end times on sale at the school library. The book was written during World War II and claimed that Adolf Hitler was the Antichrist. It also said that the second coming would happen any day.

As I looked through the book, I wondered how many Christians might have been misled to shape their lives and finances around this apocalyptic announcement.

FREEDOM PRINCIPLE
**If you read any Christian book predicting
an economic collapse, also read
2 Thessalonians.**

On my radio show I often receive calls asking me to comment on the latest gloom-and-doom book. My first response is to refer the callers to the book of 2 Thessalonians, since the early church at Thessalonica was facing some of the same problems the church is facing today.

The attitude of these early Christians was one of great anticipation of the second coming. Their hope for Christ's return was so overwhelming that the apostle Paul wrote that some of them had become busybodies and gossips. Some Christians were so convinced the end was near that they neglected their day-to-day responsibilities and their jobs. That's why Paul admonished them, "If anyone will not work, neither let him eat" (2 Thessalonians 3:10). Second Thessalonians teaches us that stewardship and financial responsibility are commanded regardless of whether we believe in the soon return of the Lord.

FINANCIAL COLLAPSES AND OUR NATIONAL DEBT

FREEDOM PRINCIPLE
No one really knows what conditions would create a financial collapse.

Many Christian leaders I have spoken with have challenged my call to calmness by asking the question, "How can you ignore the national debt? Will the United States not have to face a collapse if we keep outspending our income as a nation?" There is no question that this country cannot indefinitely spend more money than we receive in tax revenue. I believe strongly that this problem will produce dire consequences if our elected leaders do not take control. The facts examined closely, however, provide a different story than the one most commonly told.

Although it is true that a growing national debt and deficit are dangerous, they may look far more ominous than they are in reality. Many of the assumptions used in predicting an economic collapse do not take into consideration the fact that the U.S. economy is growing in terms of gross domestic product at a rate fast enough to absorb most of the negative impact of current deficits.

MANIPULATION OF THE FACTS

One of the better-known gloom-and-doom authors recently appeared in a television program and used a graphic to illustrate how bad off financially the United States will be within the next three or four years. The graphic showed all the states west of the Mississippi colored in and the statement "Soon it will take all of the tax revenue of these U.S. residents to just pay the interest on the national debt." The apparent reason this was done was to overstate the facts. Because the overwhelming population of the country lives *east* of the Mississippi, this illustration makes things look much worse than they really are. If your facts are credible, why use these kinds of tricks to make your point?

FREEDOM PRINCIPLE
**Anytime you hear extraordinary
predictions, look for extraordinary
evidence to back it up.**

In science, it is standard practice to expect a greater amount of evidence when the claim being made is extraordinary. For example, it would take much more compelling evidence to convince a scientist of the existence of flying saucers than to persuade someone that the Tampa Bay Buccaneers will have a winning season (some Tampa Bay residents may disagree with my analysis).

My point is that it is extremely fair to question statements like "The U.S. economy will collapse if . . ." and "This country could never function with that amount of debt." Why do we take these statements as fact? Where are the validating proofs for these conclusions? Predicting 10 to 15 years into the future our economic growth rate and the amount of tax revenue created and the amount of deficit and debt our country will have is highly complex. Someone would need overwhelming evidence to support these claims and some highly respected credentials to lean on.

HOW SHOULD WE PREPARE?

If you want to read a more economically profound dissertation on the economics of deficit spending, I recommend *Exploding the Doomsday Money Myths,* by Dr. Sherman Smith (Thomas Nelson, 1993). The key question of the day is: Even if the doomsday prophets are right, what should we do about it? Without question, the most destructive aspect of these books is their financial advice. If they simply stayed in the realm of macroeconomics, they would only frighten people. However, most doomsday authors cannot resist the temptation to advise people how to build a financial bomb shelter. Some of the skewed advice includes buying gold coins, liquidating retirement plans to pay off debt (this includes losing more than 50% of the value of such accounts in most cases because of taxes and penalties), storing canned goods in the cellar, and so on.

There is a huge difference between this kind of extreme advice (which is based on someone's ability to accurately predict future events), and advice that makes good common sense in response to current economic trends. For example, there is nothing wrong with *Money Magazine, The Wall Street Journal,* or other publications giving advice on making money in troubling stock markets or in times of high inflation. While it makes sense to respond to current market and economic conditions, it is not wise to make financial decisions when a specific set of future predictions are required to come true for your strategy to be profitable.

FREEDOM PRINCIPLE
**Never liquidate retirement plans because
of gloom-and-doom books.**

One of the most compelling reasons not to follow the financial advice of the doomsayers is the lack of logic inherent in their advice of how to be prepared for such events. As in giving advice on how to prepare for a nuclear holocaust, the predictions of economic meltdown are so dramatic in scope that there would be no logical preplanned investment strategy that could possibly create a winning outcome for anyone.

Let's examine a couple of the better-known recommendations.

1. **Liquidate retirement plans to pay off home mortgage and other debt.** If I were predicting that the U.S. government would fail to meet its Treasury obligations, why would I advise my followers to pay off real estate mortgages? It would seem far more logical to advise the complete liquidation of U.S. real estate and formulate a plan to buy back into the market after the collapse. Furthermore, liquidation of these retirement plans (which are primarily invested in either government and corporate bonds or stocks) include the following tax implications:

   A. A 10% excise tax (if you are younger than 59 1/2 years old).

   B. Distribution taxed as ordinary income by the federal government and by states with income tax laws. An example would be a $100,000 retirement plan reduced to $50,000 for the sake of paying off a home that purportedly will decline dramatically in value anyway.

2. **Purchase hard assets.** Numismatic dealers have used the proposition of an economic collapse artfully to make sales of their wares. After all, gold coins will be in high demand after the collapse, won't they? But gold has only occasionally lived up to its overstated reputation. The first part of the nineties gave us a war and a recession, and how did gold investors do? As poorly as they had done in the previous five to ten years.

FREEDOM PRINCIPLE
Invest no more than 10% of
your portfolio in gold.

Although gold has sometimes provided a hedge of sorts against economic uncertainty in the past, I don't really see this investment principle continuing into the next millennium. After all, our currency is not based on a gold standard any more (this is also true of many other modernized economies in the world). The concept that gold is a "store of last value" is certainly arguable. The idea that our technologically, nearly cashless society is still looking to gold and other precious metals as a "store of last value" is not true at all. Not only has gold not responded to economic and military crises as it once did, but it is no longer even a standard for valuing the currency of the United States.

Richard Nixon made a much-criticized decision in the early seventies to take the United States off the "gold standard." Although the inflation of the seventies was partly blamed on this, there is really no evidence that free-floating currencies are not just as respected as when they were backed by gold. The "gold standard" may still be needed by Third World countries to serve as a confidence-builder to encourage foreign investment, but is cetainly not needed in our ATM-and-computer-based banking system of the twenty-first century.

FREEDOM PRINCIPLE
The best way to prepare for an economic
collapse is to simply continue with a
solid financial plan.

Let's assume an economic collapse is imminent. What should you do? The surprising answer to this question is: *Nothing different from what you would do otherwise.*

1. Plan to become debt-free.
2. Build adequate cash reserves.
3. Invest for your family's future, using a diversified approach, including:
   A. Mutual funds (U.S. and international);
   B. Real estate (your own home and perhaps a limited amount of rental real estate);
   C. Government bonds, notes, and bills;
   D. Variable annuities, etc. (more in Chapter 11).

Are you surprised? The only logical plan of action I can think of comes from an honest "what if" scenario considering both good and bad economic climates. The same sound financial principles that we would otherwise follow are also appropriate even with the spector of an economic collapse.

FREEDOM PRINCIPLE
There is no strategy that will guarantee a
positive result for you if a catastrophic
economic collapse occurs.

There is virtually no investment or personal finance strategy that can logically claim to benefit from the collapse of the U.S. economy. The stress on both our economy and our entire social and political structure would be so immense that there would be a negative impact on every possible investment strategy imaginable. The value of real estate, stocks, gold, and mutual funds (for that matter, any investment) is based on what someone else is willing to pay for what you have. For those that have money, I'm sure that food and shelter will be a much greater priority than gold in a time of sheer panic created by the the loss of international credibility of the United States, the world's financial superpower.

But let's suppose you decide to liquidate your retirement plans and discontinue funding your own retirement investments plus those earmarked for your children's education. If after doing all this the economy does *not* collapse, you will have lost much of what it took years for you to acquire. And there will be no way to reverse your decision at that point.

As you can see, placing all your bets on gloom-and-doom prophecies is extremely risky. While I do not believe that we should ignore our government's deficit spending problem, I think we can use our nervous energy more wisely by contacting our elected representatives to stop them from overspending, which is the real problem in the first place.

Will there be an economic collapse? It's possible, but my standard of evidence is simply too high to accept these "Chicken Little" predictions. Most of the people making these predictions have been doing so inaccurately for years now, and the United States is still unquestionably the most resilient and expanding economy in the history of the world. For example, many people predicted economic collapses in troubling times like the oil embargo of the seventies or the 20% interest rates in the early eighties. In both instances they were completely wrong.

Remember the parable of the talents (Matthew 25:14–30)? In that parable we saw two different approaches to stewardship: either taking what we have been blessed with and making the most of it by investing it to grow, or "burying our money in the ground" in our financial bomb shelter. Investing, and not burying, is the will of God even in our times.

3

ARE YOU COVERED?

Most people who have followed my career know that the genesis of James Paris as a Christian consumer advocate was triggered by an experience my family had with an insurance company. To this day, I'm sure the company doesn't know it "created a monster" that may haunt it and its industry for the next several decades. I grew up in a small suburb on the south side of Chicago. My family and I lived in a middle-class, blue-collar neighborhood. My father was a union electrician, and was in the trade before his eighteenth birthday. One ordinary day I came home from high school on the school bus, and after I was dropped off I walked up the same street that I had hundreds of times before. However, this day would be different.

Standing in the doorway of our two-story brick home was my mother, who informed me that my father had been in a construction accident earlier that day. What most of us thought would be a minor, easy-to-recover from injury turned into a ten-year episode of 13 hospital stays and three life-or-death surgeries on my father's lower back to relieve a buildup of pressure on his spinal cord. When I tell this story on my radio broadcasts or seminars, the reaction is always the same: Most people are extremely sympathetic and recognize what a tragedy this would be for any family.

This story gets worse, however. Only several months after my father's disabling accident, the insurance company that was paying his disability claim decided without warning that they would stop making these payments. Our family attorney informed us that this was a common business strategy, and the insurance company would now try to force our family into a position of settling for a lump sum payment so they would be released from this ongoing monthly obligation. And so at the age of 15 I began the the first of a series of full-time jobs. The money from my work helped provide groceries and financial support to my family.

Being the oldest of three children, I became a 15-year-old breadwinner. Over those years our family was blessed by the generous gifts of people in our church and our neighborhood. My father ultimately settled with the insurance company many years later and is now retired with my mother in Orlando, Florida.

My story is not unique. As a matter of fact, insurance company executives who are able to successfully apply this strategy (and thus deny a policyholder from his or her rightful claim) are often recognized at awards banquets and given plaques, trophies, and bonus checks for saving the company money. Insurance companies are in business to collect more premiums than they pay out in claims, and so they have an incredible conflict of interest. Whether you were a victim of Hurricane Andrew in South Florida and could not get the money in an expedient fashion from your homeowner's insurance company to repair your home, or whether you are among the hundreds of thousands of people whose claims are denied without justification, you will be able to relate with me and the information in this chapter.

WINNING THE INSURANCE GAME

By way of disclaimer, I must admit that I feel very challenged writing a chapter attempting to show you how to win the insurance game. I have written so many articles and appeared on so many talk shows to talk about insurance that it is about time for me to say what really needs to be said: No one can truly "win" the insurance game; the only "winners" are those people who figure out ways to lose less than others. To truly understand how to save money on insurance, we must start with a particular premise—namely, that less is better. Contrary to what the industry would like us to believe, there are circumstances where we can live without their products. In fact, at some point in our lives, with proper planning, we should have no need for many forms of insurance upon retirement, since we hopefully will be "self-insured" by then.

HOW MUCH INSURANCE DO YOU NEED?

My first national radio broadcast was unique, not only because it was the first time I would expand beyond local radio, but because my first guest was Ralph Nader. Somehow my producer was able to get him to appear as my first guest. Ralph Nader, despite his sometimes liberal political views, is generally an "advocate's advocate." In his short 20-minute interview to discuss his latest book (an insurance book), he made the point repeatedly that less is more when it comes to insurance.

Of course this was not the first time that I had heard this concept. Probably the first time I heard the anti-insurance industry stance it was from a friend of mine who began selling life insurance for A. L. Williams. Williams, a high school coach in Georgia, started his own insurance business, which soon evolved into the world's largest life insurance sales force. Art Williams was not shy about his campaign to stop America's life insurance giants from "soaking" the little guy.

I began to realize very early in my career that there were two viewpoints on insurance, one coming from big insurance companies and the other from those who are insurance industry outsiders. Such statements as "You can never have too much insurance" and "Everyone needs disability insurance" started to sound like what they were—sales pitches. I can say with complete accuracy, in interviewing hundreds of guests over the years on my television and radio shows, that the line in the sand has always been pretty clear: Those who are industry insiders want Americans to buy more and more insurance, and those who are consumer advocates present a more balanced approach, including sensible ways to live without certain insurance products. In this chapter we will discuss numerous ways to save money on insurance, but to begin with I will help you develop a money-saving mentality when it comes to insurance. To do this, I would like to impart to you my three core beliefs about insurance, which I give in the next three Freedom Principles.

FREEDOM PRINCIPLE
You cannot insure every possible risk in your life.

Many agents use a simple sales tactic: They show a prospect an area of risk he or she has, and the prospect automatically buys coverage. For example; "Have you considered the fact that you might become disabled, or even need nursing home care?" The way the game goes is simple: The agent finds a risk you agree exists and then you buy insurance to cover it, because you have been led to believe that it is not responsible to let any risk go uninsured. The only way to defend yourself against these sales tactics is to realize that our lives are filled with numerous financial risks, and most of us simply do not have enough money, even if we used every last penny we have, to buy all of the insurance we "need."

There are essentially three ways of dealing with risk.

1. **Risk transfer.** This is the process by which we pay someone else, traditionally an insurance company, to take the risk for us (premature death, car accident, house fire, etc.).

2. **Risk avoidance.** This is the process by which we avoid risks that otherwise might cause us loss (parking our car in a well-lit parking lot, buying a home outside a flood plain or earthquake-prone area, not smoking, not driving in dangerous weather, etc.).
3. **Risk retention.** Not buying insurance to cover a particular type of risk is the primary way we can save big money on insurance. The insurance industry, in general, considers the concept of retaining risk as foolish and irresponsible. After all, why retain a risk when you can transfer it to an insurance company and not have a financial risk at all? The real truth is that in many cases it is much more affordable and makes much more financial sense to "self-insure" for many risks and to use your own reserves (created from savings on premiums) to pay your own "claims." We will talk more about this concept later in the chapter.

FREEDOM PRINCIPLE
You can't beat the house.

Much like casinos, insurance companies have statistically stacked the odds in their favor. What this means is that in the overwhelming majority of cases you will pay far more in premiums than you will ever get back in benefits. This has to be true, since the insurance industry must collect more money in premiums than it pays out in claims or it will go broke. Although this may sound like common sense, many educated and intelligent people I have counseled do not understand this basic concept. For example, many insurance companies have been guilty over the years of selling life insurance as an investment. The State of Florida recently fined an insurance company giant for this type of misrepresentation. How can an investment be truly an investment if you most likely will not even get back your original capital? Will Rogers was once quoted as saying that he was concerned not so much with the return *on* his investment but with the return *of* his investment. Mr. Rogers must have been dealing with insurance agents!

FREEDOM PRINCIPLE
The more bells and whistles,
the worse the value.

Today when you go to a grocery store and do comparison shopping, one rule of thumb is that buying a bigger box of food gives you a better unit price. This is called "added value." The insurance industry also offers what they call "added value," but it is the reverse of what most of us are used to. Any "added value" that is attached to your insurance policy brings more value for *them* than for you. A perfect example is whole life insurance. This expensive form of life insurance is nearly ten times the cost of basic death benefit coverage (known as term life) and of course pays out five to ten times the commission to the insurance agent. Whole life insurance is simply the insurance industry's way of trying to combine the philosphies of investing and insurance in one package. While I am a proponent of both of these philosphies, I would rather purchase only basic death coverage (term life) so that I can make investments that will almost certainly outperform the so-called cash accumulation account inside a whole life insurance contract.

FREEDOM PRINCIPLE
The cash value in a whole life insurance
contract is really never yours.

The most compelling reason not to combine your life insurance and investments through whole life insurance is that the investment is really not for you but for the insurance company.

If you purchase a whole life insurance policy with a death benefit of $100,000 and have made premium payments long enough to also have accumulated $50,000 in the so-called internal investment account, what do your beneficiaries get when they die? Not $150,000 but just the original $100,000 that you were insured for! What happened to the $50,000? The insurance company keeps it. Even if you take some of this money out during your lifetime, you must agree to pay it back to them as a loan. The insurance industry has gotten away with this misleading and unfair practice for over 100 years. It is in the contract, so read the fine print carefully.

There are other forms of so-called "cash value" life insurance which are more consumer-friendly. Coverages such as universal and variable life do in fact give you "real" ownership of the internal accumulation account, unlike whole life. Although these are improvements, they are just improvements on a bad idea. You will not get taken advantage of to the same degree by these coverages, but they are still filled with expenses and do not provide the investment potential of noninsurance alternatives such as mutual funds.

Other "bells and whistles" that can cost you big money are unneeded coverages like "double indemnity." This coverage provides your beneficiary with twice the benefit if you die in an accident. But why would you need to have more money available to your family because the cause of your death was accidental rather than from natural causes? Of course you don't. This is simply another way for the insurance industry to reach deeper into your pockets.

WAYS TO SAVE MONEY ON INSURANCE

The insurance industry has created many different types of insurance. The challenge for us is to make sure we aren't buying more insurance than we really need. Let's look at the kinds of insurance that we *don't* need (and save money in the process!).

TERM LIFE INSURANCE AND A MUTUAL FUND VS. WHOLE LIFE INSURANCE

Year	Whole Life	Term	Net to Mutual Fund	Mutual Fund Values	Term Death Benefit	Year End Cash Values	Whole Life Death Benefit
1	2,505	240	2,265	2,491	250,000	0	250,000
2	2,505	262	2,243	5,206	250,000	0	250,000
3	2,505	284	2,220	11,397	250,000	590	250,000
4	2,505	307	2,198	13,158	250,000	2,917	250,000
5	2,505	335	2,170	14,920	250,000	5,482	250,000
6	2,505	365	2,140	18,760	250,000	8,314	250,000
7	2,505	405	2,100	22,940	250,000	11,420	250,000
8	2,505	457	2,048	27,479	250,000	14,829	250,000
9	2,505	517	1,988	32,405	250,000	18,564	250,000
10	2,505	587	1,918	37,744	250,000	22,651	250,000
11	258	1,135	-877	40,542	250,000	22,684	250,000
12	0	1,202	-1,202	43,262	250,000	26,652	250,000
13	0	1,277	-1,277	46,171	250,000	28,787	250,000
14	0	1,355	-1,355	49,283	250,000	31,103	250,000
15	0	1,437	-1,437	52,616	250,000	33,611	250,000
16	0	1,520	-1,520	56,190	250,000	36,237	250,000
17	0	1,672	-1,672	59,953	250,000	39,260	250,000
18	0	1,840	-1,840	63,906	250,000	42,417	250,000
19	0	2,022	-2,022	68,054	250,000	45,800	250,000
20	0	2,260	-2,260	72,352	250,000	49,444	250,000

The chart above illustrates the results when a 35-year-old male nonsmoker purchases whole life insurance and compares what would happen if the same person were to purchase term life insurance and invest the difference in a mutual fund with an annual return of 15 percent. The second column, titled "Whole Life," shows the cost of this type of insurance. The third column, titled "Term," shows the cost of purchasing a term policy, which is considerably cheaper. The difference, then, is invested into a mutual fund (see column four). You can compare the ultimate results by looking at how much money the mutual fund brings to the investor (bottom of column five, "Mutual Fund Values"), and the cash value accrued by the whole life policy (bottom of column seven, "Year End Cash Values"). This chart does not tell the whole story; remember that commissions on whole life insurance can be as much as ten times those of term insurance, and any withdrawal of whole life cash value is subject to surrender charges. The bottom line? Whole life insurance is not the way to go.

FREEDOM PRINCIPLE
**Do not buy a life insurance policy that
covers the loan on a consumer product.**

This type of life insurance policy is usually sold to you
when you buy a big-ticket item such as an automobile, a
refrigerator, a camcorder, and so on. The concept is simple: If
you die during the term of the financing contract, the insurance company pays off the balance of the loan.

If you follow the advice in this chapter you will already
include your need to pay off all debts upon your death in your
existing insurance plan. The one large policy that you obtain
should meet all of your personal needs and your family's needs
in the event of such a tragedy. Obtaining life insurance in such
small amounts to cover yourself in a piece-by-piece approach
is really not the best way to handle these risks. The main problem with this coverage is the expense, which is dramatically
higher than basic term.

Another rip-off is the fact that although your balance is
decreasing, your premium stays the same. Even though this
coverage may start by being ten times as expensive as basic
term life, by the end of the contract, when the balance owed
decreases, it can literally be thousands of times overpriced.
Deception is typically used to sell this coverage. Many times
the finance person of the retailer will attempt to add this coverage to your financing contract by quoting it as "only $10
extra per month." This is a high-profit item for the retailer,
and if the truth be told, more money is now being made from
financing and ridiculous add-ons like this than on the mer-
chandise being sold.

My best advice to you is to say no to credit life insurance.
If you have already purchased it, you can cancel it at any time
during the existing finance contract and thereby save the cost
of the monthly premium starting immediately. Also, many
states have enacted legislation prohibiting finance companies

(including retailers who provide financing) from telling customers that they will not be approved if they do not take the life insurance option. From a strategic standpoint, it is poor planning to buy your life insurance in small pieces rather than determining your overall need for life insurance and making the decision to buy one policy that covers all your needs.

FREEDOM PRINCIPLE
Do not purchase accident insurance.

Many people have coverage that pays a death/hospital benefit in the event of an accident. The problem here again is the piecemeal approach. Why buy a policy that will only pay off during an accident? If you need coverage for accidents, this can be included in a basic life or medical insurance policy, so why cover yourself twice? Some people may answer that they wouldn't mind enjoying double the benefit by having two if not three policies in force for the same risks. The problem with this thinking is that the insurance companies beat you again. Virtually every accident policy issued prohibits such "double dipping," so remember that since you usually can only collect once, don't pay twice. Life insurance policies are typically the only form of insurance that will pay off regardless of how many policies are in force. Your potential to collect is virtually unlimited so long as the insurance company will issue you the coverage. We will talk more about duplicate coverage later, which is one of the mechanisms that the insurance industry uses to pad their profits.

FREEDOM PRINCIPLE
Do not purchase extended warranties.

Many people would not consider extended warranties as insurance, but they are. This insurance is fast becoming a major profit source for retailers, especially electronics stores and car dealers. Again, the problem is simple: You cannot afford this coverage on everything you own. We all must draw a line somewhere in the sand and say no. Recently when I purchased a few telephone headsets for our office the salesperson vehemently tried to sell me an extended warranty that would have cost more than 20% of the headsets themselves! If one in five didn't wear out during the warranty period, I would lose on this deal. You guessed it, I said no! Saying no to insurance is a way of life for me. Because I have come to understand the principles of self-insurance, it feels good to say no and save the money. To date I have no regrets for doing so.

INSURANCE YOU WILL NEED

Auto Insurance

Auto insurance is much more complicated than it needs to be. Essentially, most auto insurance contracts cover three areas:

1. **Collision.** This covers the damage incurred by your automobile in a car accident.

2. **Comprehensive.** This section of the policy covers you in the event of theft or vandalism or other types of loss that could occur outside a typical accident in which you are driving your car (i.e., your car burns up in your garage, is destroyed by a tornado, etc.).

3. **Liability.** This is the portion of coverage that pays the property damages and medical expenses of those you have injured in an accident. Liability is usually quoted in two amounts. For example: $100,000/$300,000. This would mean that your policy limits claims payments on liability from accidents to $100,000 per *person* and $300,000 per *accident*. It also covers liability created when a passenger in your vehicle is injured from an accident you are responsible for.

INSURANCE

Auto insurance is not an option, since most states require it, and well they should. In our litigious society the amount you can lose in an accident is virtually unlimited, and an auto insurance policy enables you to protect yourself from a catastrophic lawsuit that could cost you all your retirement and investment savings.

While it is necessary for you to have auto insurance, there are a number of ways you can trim your costs.

FREEDOM PRINCIPLE
Drop collision and comprehensive coverages once the value of your car drops below $2000.

In states where auto insurance is required, the requirement is primarily *liability* coverage. The state wants you to be able to pay a driver you may injure in an accident and also have the financial resources to repair or replace his or her automobile. It is your option, however, whether you cover your own automobile against loss. My recommendation is to drop the collision and comprehensive coverages once you determine that your car is worth $2000 or less. This coverage can be so expensive that it makes no financial sense to insure for such a small amount.

FREEDOM PRINCIPLE
Purchase liability coverage at a discount.

One little-known strategy is to buy the minimum required amount of liability coverage from your insurance company and then purchase the balance of coverage as umbrella liability. Personal liability policies (known as umbrella liability) can be purchased for outrageously modest sums. For example, I have purchased $1,000,000 of umbrella liability for less than $300 per year! The way umbrella liability works is simple: Once the liability limits run out on your homeowner's and/or auto insurance, this policy covers the amounts in excess of those limits. In our example above, let's say you have a 100/300 liability policy limit (that is, $100,000 maximum coverage per person and $300,000 maximum per accident). If you wish to do so, you can increase your overall liability to $1,300,000 for an additional $300 or so per year. My suggestion is to buy at least enough coverage to equal two times your net worth. Frankly, since a million is so inexpensive, I would consider this as a minimum for anyone.

FREEDOM PRINCIPLE
Raise your deductible to lower the
cost of your policy.

Raising the deductible on your auto insurance policy is a form of risk retention. If you could retain just a small amount of the risk your auto policy is now covering, how much could you save? Based on my experience, a large amount. The average policy cost will decrease by 25% when the deductible is raised to $500 and by 50% when raised to $1000! Unless you have an accident every year, you are probably better off carrying higher deductibles. This is true because the higher premium cost will easily exceed the cost of the deductible every 12 to 18 months (even if you had to file a claim every year and a half).

FREEDOM PRINCIPLE
Don't underestimate the value
of shopping around.

Usually all it takes to comparison shop is to call two or three major insurance companies each year to see if you can get a better deal. The following companies have been among the most competitive in recent years:

USAA	1-800-531-8319
Erie Insurance Exchange	1-800-458-0811
Geico	1-800-841-3000
Liberty Mutual	(see yellow pages for local office)
Prudential	1-800-368-8868
Nationwide Mutual	(see yellow pages for local office)

FREEDOM PRINCIPLE
**Drop "bells-and-whistles" coverage but
maintain uninsured-motorist coverage.**

Take out your policy and look for coverage that you do not need. Examples include: towing and the use of a rental car while your car is being serviced from an accident. While eliminating these nonessentials, be careful not to cut too deeply. Such coverages as uninsured-motorist and medical coverage for you should be considered necessities. A well-known financial expert has been telling people for years to drop the uninsured-motorist portion of their coverage. His position is that the uninsured-motorist coverage would duplicate other coverages you already have. To some degree he is right, since the collision portion of your policy would pay off if the other driver couldn't pay and the medical coverage of your policy would pay your medical expenses. However, without uninsured-motorist coverage you cannot seek compensation for disability, dismemberment (loss of an arm or leg), loss of life, and loss of future earnings from employment. Uninsured-motorist coverage allows you to collect from your insurance company the same amount that a court would find the uninsured motorist liable for up to your policy limits. If you become disabled and cannot continue in your career, or are killed, you could have a claim worth millions of dollars, and rightfully so.

FREEDOM PRINCIPLE
**Be sure to ask about any discounts
which may apply to you.**

If you have more than one car insured, or if you have not had an accident in a long time, or if you are a senior citizen or a good student, you may be entitled to a discount from your insurance company. Generally you will find these discounts more often than they find you. By this I mean that most agents will not voluntarily point out these special offers; you must ask for them.

If your child starts driving at the age of 16 or 17, the risks can be great and the insurance will be expensive. The occasional-driver clause in your insurance policy will not cover your child's driving, since he or she is more than an occasional driver according to the insurance company's standards. He will need to purchase his own coverage or be added to your policy (adding him or her to your own policy makes sense if he is going to be driving the family car).

In most states, drivers under the age of 25 face unbelievably expensive coverage. This is especially true for males. The insurance industry has legally discriminated against male drivers for years by charging them higher rates, especially when they are young. From an asset-protection standpoint, you should realize that your teen is a dangerous source of liability for you because, if he is driving your car, you will most likely be named in any legal action along with him as the driver if he becomes involved in an accident. One solution to this is to help your child buy a used car and have the car titled in his or her name. If the car is older (ten years old or more), it could be very affordable and also would not require collision and comprehensive coverage, since its value would be below $2000, as stated before. However, this strategy may not totally relieve you of all liability, since some states have now passed parental responsibility laws that make parents of minor children their full partner in any liability they incur. In other words, the claimant would sue both you and your child if the law so allows. This is an important issue to discuss with your family attorney, since laws vary from state to state. Insuring against the risk of teenage drivers can be tricky, and certainly nothing to take lightly. One thing is certain: A good lawyer will name *both* the driver and owner in a lawsuit.

Life Insurance

Life insurance, incorrectly named, should really be called *death* insurance, since that is what it does: It pays off when you die. Life insurance is a contract between an individual and an insurance company. The contract requires that the policy owner (you) pay an insurance company premiums to pay a person (beneficiary) whom you select an agreed amount (death benefit) upon your death. Life insurance companies have become some of the most wealthy institutions in America. They have created their wealth using "OPM"—other people's money. In this chapter I have referred to the concept of *term* life insurance. "Term" simply means that you are buying the insurance for a specific period of time. These time periods (terms) are usually one year. This is typically referred to as annual term, or if it is automatically renewable it would be called annual renewable term.

These insurance industry terms can sometimes get confusing, so for now simply remember that life insurance generally falls into two broad categories: term and cash value. For review purposes, cash value insurance is the combination of a term life policy with an internal investment, usually called a cash accumulation account or cash value. As stated previously, both investing and buying an appropiate amount of life insurance are good things to do. The problem created by insurance companies is that these combinations in their products result in substantial fees and commissions for them and reduced benefits to you.

FREEDOM PRINCIPLE
Don't buy cash value life insurance;
instead buy term life insurance and
invest the difference in premium
in mutual funds.

My advice is simple: Buy term life insurance in amounts appropriate for your circumstances and invest as much as you can in mutual funds. This will allow you and your family to much more rapidly reach financial independence and not just become another contributor to the already wealthy insurance industry.

FREEDOM PRINCIPLE
Obtain a death benefit of ten times
your annual income.

One question asked frequently is: How much life insurance is enough? Generally, if you obtain ten times your annual income in death benefit coverage, your family can invest these funds at about 8% to 10% per year and your income would be replaced. For example, if you earn $40,000 per year you should probably obtain about $400,000 in life insurance.

FREEDOM PRINCIPLE
Insure a nonworking spouse for ten times
the annual expense of replacing her (or
his) domestic services.

If you and your family enjoy the luxury of one spouse being able to stay home with the children and perform other domestic services, be careful to account for the economic value of these services and insure yourself against this risk. For example, my wife, Ann, does a wonderful job staying at home with our children and generally keeps our house going. In case something were to happen to her, we have purchased a life insurance policy for $300,000 on her life. The thinking is that I could invest this sum at 10% so that it would generate about $30,000 per year for a nanny/domestic services worker to be hired.

Much of how the insurance industry gets away with the deceptions described throughout this chapter has to do with the powerful insurance lobby on Capitol Hill. The insurance industry has without question enjoyed a special relationship with Washington, and has had very favorable tax and other laws passed over the years by using highly paid lobbyists. Much of this has now changed, however. In 1986 the special tax treatment of single premium life insurance that allowed investors to almost avoid taxation altogether was dealt a fatal blow. The provisions even allowed for tax-free withdrawals from the account by calling them loans rather than distributions. These rules were ostensibly wiped out by the tax reform act of 1986. Life insurance, as an investment now forced to play on a level playing field, cannot stand up to the competition. (The playing field is still somewhat tilted, since the insurance lobby is not dead, only weakened.)

Though life insurance is a very much needed and integral part of any practical financial plan, each of us needs to be very careful where we get our advice, since the insurance industry has far too much self-interest at stake to provide objective advice on the topic.

In 1994 I formed a company that assists consumers in shopping for the best term life insurance policies. We use a computer service that allows us to shop over 173 insurance companies offering term products. This computerized shopping approach can save you a substantial amount of money, as term premiums can vary greatly from company to company. The savings you can realize from converting from whole life insurance to term is large, sometimes as much as a 90% discount. Additionally, by annually shopping your term life insurance coverage you can be sure that you are getting the best possible value within the realm of simple term coverage.

As a reader of this book, feel free to use my insurance shopping service absolutely free. Call 1-800-877-2022.

INSURANCE

4

HOW TO
BORROW WISELY

Credit cards. You may have no money in your pocket and none in your bank account, but if you have a credit card you can live a life of luxury . . . for awhile. Credit limits of several thousand dollars are more than common, and if you have had a solid payment history the credit card company (read: the bank) will reward you by raising your credit limit even further. Yes, you too can live the life of the "beautiful people" so gaudily displayed in the television commercials for these same cards. Buy now, pay later. What a grand way to go!

The trouble is, these commercials don't seem to spend much time telling you how you're ultimately going to pay for this lavish lifestyle. You *did* know you were going to have to pay for it at some time, didn't you? While credit card advertisers probably couldn't fairly be described as engaging in deceptive practices, the constant bombardment of "money for nothing" imagery might be considered unethical by some people.

My own stance could be described as something like this: While the credit card companies might be guilty of accentuating only the positives of owning their respective pieces of plastic, I don't know how really "wrong" that is. Any company that has a product deemed legal for sale should have the right to advertise that product, and I don't know how realistic it is for us as consumers to expect that this advertising will focus on anything but the positive aspects of the product. As a result, I believe that the consumer has a responsibility to himself to ensure that he understands everything about the product or service he is purchasing *before* he enters into the sale or agreement.

The thinking on this subject is debated by us as a nation these days: What is the responsibility of these companies (or the government, for that matter) to save us from ourselves? Does not the ultimate responsibility for such transactions rest squarely on the shoulders of the consumer? My answer to that is yes, as long as there is full and fair *disclosure* on the part of the company in question.

You see, disclosure is the other side of the coin here. While I don't believe that a company has an obligation to riddle its promotional advertising with warnings and other cautionary messages, any potentially harmful effects which may arise from the *use* of that product or service should be made known to the consumer at some point before the transaction takes place (or should at least be made readily available when such an inquiry is made by the consumer).

FREEDOM PRINCIPLE
Count the costs carefully before signing
up for your next credit card.

Disclosure had been a problematic issue for credit card consumers until fairly recently. For the longest time, credit card issuers were not required to disclose much information about the costs of the card *until* you received your card from the company. This outrageous practice was made to change only recently. The change came in the form of the Fair Credit and Charge Card Disclosure Act of 1988, a part of the well-known Truth-in-Lending Act. The "bottom line" of the Fair Credit and Charge Card Disclosure Act is that card issuers must clearly provide all of the relevant information about the costs of the card up-front to applicants.

If you've recently read the back of a credit card application you will undoubtedly have noticed the nice, neat box which clearly indicates the information relating to the cost of the card. That box is there as a result of the 1988 legislation, and is known informally as the "Schumer Box." It is so named for the legislator (New York Congressman Charles Schumer) who was instrumental in the passage of the bill through both Houses. Again, now that full and fair disclosure is a part of the credit card application process, consumers no longer have any reason to look elsewhere for someone to blame if they don't like the deal they have received.

The key, then, is to educate yourself as much as possible on the mechanics of how credit cards work, and how to use them wisely. During many of my travels I continue to encounter people who seem to lack a real understanding of just what a credit card is and how it works. Let's take a look, then, at the basics of credit cards.

HOW CREDIT CARDS WORK

A credit card is actually an instrument through which you can obtain an unsecured loan. Unsecured means that the money you borrow is not backed up by any specific property you own. An automobile loan is a good example of a *secured* loan; the money you borrow to pay for the vehicle is secured by the vehicle itself. Since the vehicle is pledged as a guarantee, if you fall behind on your payments, the bank will repossess the vehicle. Unsecured debt, however, is not backed up by anything but your word. The only thing that the credit card issuer really has to hold on to as far as being repaid is the integrity and creditworthiness of the consumer.

Credit cards like Visa and MasterCard are actually issued through banks; in other words, there is no such thing as a Visa card issued directly by Visa. Instead, that Visa card is actually issued by a bank. Visa is an association that provides the logistical and administrative support to the huge number of banks who actually issue the cards and who provide the financial means to the credit card carrier and the merchant. That's why you can apply for Visas and MasterCards with widely varying terms; the terms are set by the individual lenders, not by the Visa and MasterCard associations.

One of the hallmarks of such bank-issued credit cards (or bank cards, as they are known) is that they allow you to carry a *revolving* line of credit. Revolving means that you are permitted to carry a balance on your card from one month to the next. This is where discussions of interest rates become important. Called a "finance charge" by the credit card issuers, the interest rate is what you pay back to the bank for allowing you to borrow the money in the first place. If a credit card carries a finance charge of 18% per year (known as 18% APR—Annual Percentage Rate), this means that the monthly rate is 1.5%. An interest rate of 1.5% per month may not sound like a lot, but what it means in real dollars can be very significant if you carry a sizable balance from month to month. If you have a $2000 balance on your card in a given month, the interest which will accumulate that month will be $30. Calculate that monthly figure for a full year and you will see that the interest charges on that $2000 alone would add up to $360. That 1.5% per month doesn't seem so insignificant now, does it?

I would now like to explain the difference between credit cards and charge cards. Most people tend to lump the two together in discussion, but there is a key difference: A charge card is an instrument that also allows you to make purchases and incur expenses, but with a charge card *you must pay off your balance in full each month*. These charge cards are also known as travel-and-entertainment cards, although that phrase is curious because it in no way seems to imply that you must pay off your balance each month.

But can you not use a Visa or MasterCard for travel and entertainment purposes? Of course you can. The real benefit to carrying a charge card (the best-known of these is the American Express card) is that there is no set spending limit. You can charge whatever you want, within reason. Remember, though, that the balance is *due to be paid in full each month*. Also, you may find the annual fees charged by such travel-and-entertainment cards to be quite a bit higher than those charged by credit cards, for this simple reason: Without providing you with a revolving line of credit, and therefore a running balance against which a finance charge may be assessed, the charge card company must find other ways to increase its profitability.

MANAGING CREDIT CARDS WISELY

FREEDOM PRINCIPLE
**Always use a no-annual-fee credit card if
you pay off your balance each month.**

Typically, charge cards assess fairly high annual fees. The way to get around this problem is to get a no-annual-fee Visa or Mastercard and pay off the balance each month *as if* it were a requirement. Remember, the interest rates (finance charges) assessed by the Visa and MasterCard issuers apply only to balances carried from month to month. If you pay off your whole balance within each 30-day period, you'll never see a finance charge.

True, without the travel-and-entertainment card you won't have the benefit of the unrestricted spending limit, but how prudent a feature is that anyway? For many people, such a "benefit" could be an invitation to disaster. The level of competition among credit card issuers is quite intense, so it shouldn't be too difficult to find a no-annual-fee card which would be happy to have you as a holder. Furthermore, if you're the sort of person who feels he must pay his debts fully each month, your payment history (and thus your credit record) is probably outstanding, so approval for such cards should pose little challenge.

FREEDOM PRINCIPLE
Don't purchase any goods or services
with a credit card which you cannot
pay off within 30 days.

This could be considered the second part of the previous Freedom Principle, but it does need some explaining. First of all, I am not suggesting that you buy nothing which you cannot pay for completely within 30 days. Many of us cannot pay for a house in much less than 30 years, let alone 30 days. I'm not talking about items like houses, cars, living room sets, and other such major expenditures. However, don't lose sight of this fact: For many people, credit cards represent a way for them to buy something which they otherwise couldn't afford. Ask yourself this question: "If there were no such things as credit cards, how could I buy something which I can't afford?" The answer is obvious—you couldn't! Get yourself in the habit of thinking through the following four-step process whenever you contemplate making a purchase with a credit card.

Step 1: Reevaluate how much you truly want or "need" the item or service.

Step 2: If you decide to go ahead with the purchase, determine if you have enough money available in your checking account to cover the cost.

Step 3: If you do have enough money available in your checking account, make the purchase with a check or a debit card. If not, determine whether you will be able to pay off the purchase within

30 days. If so, allow yourself to make the purchase with the credit card.

Step 4: If you determine you cannot pay for the purchase within 30 days, reevaluate again the pru-
dency of the purchase *before* committing to the
transaction.

I don't mean for you to deprive yourself of goods or services which you truly need, but if you get in the habit of buying items which you cannot afford, what have you really done
for yourself?

FREEDOM PRINCIPLE
Use a debit card instead of a credit card
whenever possible.

In Step 3 of the four-step process mentioned above is
something called a debit card. A debit card is an instrument
which looks just like a credit card, except that whenever you
use it the money for your purchase comes straight out of your
checking account. This, of course, is just the opposite of a
credit card. With a credit card, the amount of your purchase
is posted on your account and grows in size with the finance
charge assessed by the credit card issuer *until* you pay off the
entire balance.

Debit cards are being issued increasingly by banks, and
they work no differently from your personal checks: When the
voucher from the debit card transaction reaches your bank,
the money comes directly out of your account. The beauty of
the debit card itself is that it looks no different in appearance
than a regular Visa credit card. The merchant simply rings up
your purchase as he would normally, and you're on your way.

There are several advantages to using a debit card. First,
it allows you to tap into your checking account anywhere that

Visa is accepted. If you are far from home, you can use the debit card for purchases where you would otherwise be unable to use a personal check. Second, it allows you to feel like you are using a credit card, if that sort of thing is important to you, without having to go into debt. Third, and most important, relying on a debit card means you can't dig yourself into a huge "debt hole" from which it might be difficult to extricate yourself. As long as you remember to enter your purchases in your checkbook each time you make one, you should be all right.

FREEDOM PRINCIPLE
Do not carry more than three credit cards without good reason.

I should probably say "Do not carry more than three credit cards" and leave it at that, but I like to word these Freedom Principles in such a way that they can be as universally applicable as possible. My point is this: If you accept the notion that credit cards represent a way for you to buy what you cannot afford, and therefore you commit to using them only for large, necessary purchases as well as emergencies and travel expenses, how many do you need? I never cease to be amazed when I run across people who think nothing of carrying four or five credit cards and maintaining high balances (I'm talking thousands of dollars) on each of them. Whenever I meet someone like that, I know I'm speaking to a person who is clearly spending beyond his means. How do I know? Simple: If that person could truly afford these goods to begin with, he wouldn't have to charge them. Carrying more than one credit card just seems to be too much of a temptation to get into trouble. I do think it could be appropriate for both you and your spouse to each have a card, at least to help you in case of emergencies and other unexpected expenses.

If, after reading this, you agree that carrying only one credit card is appropriate, do what you must to get to that point: Apply a portion of any available disposable income you have at the end of each month toward paying off one of your cards. Once that one is successfully paid off, go to the next one. Keep on going until you find yourself with only one card remaining.

FREEDOM PRINCIPLE
Do not purchase any perishable goods with a credit card.

I saw a MasterCard commercial on television recently which talked about how wonderful an idea it was to use your card for paying the weekly grocery bill. Are they kidding? One of the worst uses of a credit card is to pay for perishable items. Do you really want to pay interest on your grocery bill? What about those dinners out with the family? Do you want to pay interest on those as well? The problem is that you now find yourself paying interest on something which you have consumed and is long gone. Does that make sense to you? Again, the way to circumvent this kind of mess is to stick to the view that credit cards are tools of last resort. As long as you do that, you shouldn't have any problems.

FREEDOM PRINCIPLE
Never complete a credit card application unless you fully understand the terms and your responsibilities to the issuer.

Now I realize that some of you may be somewhat insulted by the above Freedom Principle. After all, does anyone really need to be told to read a contract before he signs it? Well, when it comes to credit cards, the answer is frequently *yes*. The reason for this is that with the prevalence of these items in society, combined with the slick promotional campaigns designed to get you to gobble up more of them, you the consumer find yourself at times thinking of credit card applications as being something less than what they really are: applications for an unsecured line of credit.

As long as you regard any credit card application as a loan application, then you will probably find yourself paying much closer attention to the particulars. What is the finance charge? 9%? 10%? 16%? 21%? Take a sample figure for a balance amount, say $1000, and calculate what that interest rate does to your balance on a *monthly* basis. Will the issuer assess late fees if you fail to pay the minimum monthly payment on time? Is there a special, higher interest rate you must pay when you use your credit card to obtain a cash advance? Thanks to the legislative process, these pieces of information are easy to locate now; they're all on your credit card application. Don't assume that all credit cards are basically the same. The fact is that many have little in common besides their appearance. It's up to you to do your homework.

FREEDOM PRINCIPLE
**Shop around for a low-interest
credit card.**

It should be clear to you by now that all credit cards are *not* created equal. One advantage to being a consumer in a market flooded with credit cards is that there naturally exists a climate of competition. Banks make money by making loans, so they can charge interest. This competition, however, results in the existence of some cards which charge less interest than others.

With the availability of such cards, it makes sense that you shop around to find the card offering the best deal. The "best deal" might be a low interest rate, no annual fee, or both. To give you some kind of perspective on what to look for, let's see what you should expect as far as interest rates are concerned.

The interest rate, or finance charge, assessed by the bank will reflect where interest rates currently are throughout the United States and with lending institutions as a whole. When interest rates are low, credit card rates will also be low. When interest rates are on the rise, however, credit card rates will naturally follow suit. The key, then, is to understand where interest rates stand within the broad economy and how they are reflected by credit cards.

For example, if the Prime Rate (the leading interest rate indicator) is at 6%, then you will probably find credit cards which charge rates as low as 6% or 7%. Basically, you should take the current Prime Rate and add 1% to 2% to it to get the range within which the lowest-rate cards should be falling. If the Prime Rate is at 8%, does it make sense for you to settle for a card which charges an APR (Annual Percentage Rate) of 19%? I would suggest that you get an idea of where the Prime Rate is at currently (consult your newspaper's business section) and begin to look for cards which charge APRs in the range I discussed. A good way to stay up-to-date on bank card interest rates is to subscribe to my monthly newsletter, the James L. Paris *Perspective*. I publish a record of the available low-interest credit cards in each issue. To become a subscriber, call 1-800-877-2022.

Remember, don't settle for just any credit card. Do the comparison shopping necessary to get you the best deal.

FREEDOM PRINCIPLE
**If you can't get approved for an
unsecured credit card, apply for a
secured credit card.**

Although I've spent a good portion of this chapter focusing on the negative aspects of credit cards, it should be said that they clearly have their benefits. First, a credit card is great to have in emergencies. Few merchants anywhere won't honor Visa and MasterCard, and by having a credit card with you at all times you will always have a source of emergency money. Second, credit cards make great travel companions. It's never a good idea to carry large sums of cash with you on vacation, and even if you take traveler's checks, a credit card serves as a nice backup. Third, a credit card gives you a way to build a high-quality credit record where none may previously exist. Credit and your own personal creditworthiness will play large roles in your life as a consumer, and having a record of successful payments to a credit card account will go a long way to ensuring that you are approved for such sizable loan ventures as a home mortgage and an automobile loan.

Sometimes, however, it can be difficult to gain approval for an unsecured, or "regular," credit card if you have no credit record to review. The answer, then, is a *secured* credit card. A secured credit card is also a bank card, but with a twist: You deposit a sum of money into a certificate of deposit at the issuing bank, and your credit limit on the card is equal to the amount of money you've deposited. The better deals in secured cards now offer you 150% of your deposit as a credit line. For example, if you deposit $1000 to get a secured card, your credit line would actually be $1500.

One nice thing about a secured card is that it looks no different from any other Visa or MasterCard. The merchant will not be able to tell that your card is secured, and to be honest, it really doesn't matter anyway. Furthermore, once you've held the card for at least a year with no problems, most banks will allow you to petition them to have the status changed to unsecured, thereby enhancing your creditworthiness even further. You will find a list of sources for secured credit cards located at the back of this book in Appendix A.

ELIMINATING CREDIT CARD DEBT

While it is always best to never let your credit card spending get away from you in the first place, a great many of us are burdened with leftover debt from days when we thought living well involved nothing more than emulating our favorite characters from credit card commercials. So what is the best way to go about reducing a sizable amount of credit card debt which may be found on several cards at one time?

FREEDOM PRINCIPLE
Transfer credit card balances from high-interest cards to low-interest cards.

An interesting trend I've noticed developing within the bank card industry is the encouragement on the part of credit card issuers to have you receive *their* particular low-interest card so that you can transfer the debt on your current card (which probably carries a higher APR) over to the new piece of plastic. The issuer will even provide you with a special set of checks which allow you to do this.

Why would they want to do this? Because credit card issuers are banks, and banks make money by lending money. If there is an interest rate to be paid, they would much rather you pay it to them than to anyone else. This appears to be a case of a "win-win" situation. First, the bank wins because they are now collecting interest from you, when before you were paying it to another issuer. Second, you win because that interest rate is now lower, maybe considerably lower. If you aren't sure how much of APR you're paying on your card(s), do some checking. Typically, anything above 15% is high, and anything above 18% is *very* high. Surprisingly, there are still many people who are paying over 20% on their credit cards! As long as you have a satisfactory payment history, you should have little trouble obtaining cards at the most competitive rates.

But there *is* something you should be aware of before you run out and start applying for low-interest cards. If you already find yourself buried under a mountain of debt, you may find that the more competitive issuers will tell you to forget it and come back when you have reduced your debt somewhat. You see, even if you've been making your minimum payments on time, any prospective new issuer will be wary of giving you the means to bury yourself even further. They realize, of course, that at some point you may not be able to continue meeting your monthly obligations. Even though *you* know that you only want this new card for balance-transfer purposes, the prospective issuers may not be willing to take any chances. They will evaluate your application relative to your current level of debt.

FREEDOM PRINCIPLE
Use a systematic method to pay down
multiple credit card balances.

What do you do when you've allowed those credit cards to get away from you and you're now facing several balances to pay on two or more cards? This is a question I've received many times throughout the years, so I can only assume that it is a fairly widespread problem. The first thing you should do when you realize that this is a problem is stay calm. Don't allow yourself to panic or to become overwhelmed by the bills which seem to be surrounding you now. The best thing to do is to lay out each of the bills in front of you and formulate a systematic plan for paying off each one of them. It's not as difficult a task as it may appear, and the key to being successful is to be patient and diligent and to stick to the plan. There are basically two paths you can take when implementing this systematic type of plan, and I've found that each can be quite successful in its own right.

The first method is known as the "highest rate" plan. This means that you organize your bills in a way which allows you to concentrate on paying down the one with the highest interest rate first, the next-highest interest rate second, and so on. To implement this plan most effectively, you should work up a monthly budget for yourself. The goal here is to try to determine how much disposable income (or "extra money") you have at the end of each month. Assuming that you're making the minimum monthly payments on each of your cards, go one step further and apply as much of that disposable income as you can to the credit card with the highest interest rate. A good rule of thumb is to divide the amount of the disposable income by three, then take one of those thirds and send it to the high-rate credit card issuer (this is, of course, in addition to the minimum payment which you're already sending them). When you have completely paid down that card, move on to the next-highest and repeat the process.

The second method is known as the "lowest balance" plan. With the "lowest balance" plan you will concentrate on paying off the card with the lowest total balance, without regard to the interest rate. The benefit to this is that you can more quickly eliminate one of your card balances, which also gives you a feeling of accomplishment. You would apply a portion of your disposable income to the card with the lowest balance in the same way you did toward the card with the highest interest rate.

I have found both of these methods to be excellent, but you must remain focused. If you happen to receive some type of unexpected windfall, perhaps in the form of a tax refund, play it smart: Apply as much of that windfall as you can toward the credit card you're paying off.

The Bible is clear: The misuse of debt will create bondage. I cannot even estimate the number of people who have called and written me after paying off their credit cards to share the news of their new-found financial freedom.

The stories of success vary; however, the approach is always the same: Ordinary people make a commitment to become debt-free. I'm not talking about a passing whim; I mean a real heartfelt commitment. They may struggle for years to scrape together just that little bit of extra money each month to stay on their course of financial freedom. Anything truly worth accomplishing will not be easy, and becoming free from credit cards is no different. Yet it can be done if you are disciplined and stay focused on the end result of breaking the financial bondage that has ensnared you. The choice is yours: You can spend the rest of your life working to pay bills, or you can be debt-free and use that money any way that God directs you to, including funding your children's college, paying for your retirement, and giving to the Lord's work.

Credit and credit cards are just financial tools. By themselves they are not good or bad; those judgments are simply a reflection of how they are used. I can take a hammer and build a house, or I can use that same hammer to smash a car windshield. My best advice is to proceed with extreme caution in your use of credit.

5

WHEN YOUR CREDIT IS IN TROUBLE

In early 1993 I started a credit repair and debt mediation company. My goal was to help people who are struggling with bad credit. Over the past couple of years I have learned a lot about credit and credit repair. Perhaps my most significant lesson was understanding how many different areas of our lives are affected by our credit reports. I had always thought of credit repair as one-dimensional in terms of the benefits that could be gained by applying these strategies.

For example, if you were going to be in need of credit, whether in obtaining a mortgage, credit card, or whatever, having clean credit is obviously a benefit. I had not realized, however, that many major employers pull credit reports before hiring prospective employees. I also never considered how much money it can cost an American family to have impaired credit.

For example, an elderly lady in her seventies was one of our first clients. We worked with her for three months, helping her to repair her credit. One day she called our office, and as she was weeping on the phone, she explained how she had refinanced her mortgage from 14% down to 7% because of her now-improved credit file. She said she lived on a fixed income, and now that she has several hundred dollars more per month in her budget, she felt she had been released from financial bondage.

Bad credit applies its own penalty to our lives in many different and expensive ways. Not only could it cause you to pay a double-digit interest rate on a mortgage, but it might also cost you a job opportunity without your even knowing it. In this chapter I will share with you insider strategies of credit repair that I have learned over the past several years, especially since starting my own credit repair and debt mediation company. The benefits you will gain by applying this information are almost unlimited, and as you will see, good credit is as important as any other aspect of personal finance.

A DOWNWARD SPIRAL

Sadly, more and more Americans declare personal bankruptcy each day. In 1991, more than one million people declared personal bankruptcy. That's more than double the figure for 1980.[1] An even larger number of Americans who are *not* faced with the sinister specter of Chapters 7 or 13 still find themselves dogged by blemishes on their credit records. What accounts for this unfortunate rise in both personal bankruptcies and tarnished credit histories?

Many of these problems can be traced to the misuse of credit cards. Every day we are bombarded in all forms of media with advertisements which speak only of the convenience afforded by credit cards. We are made to believe that, armed only with one of these precious pieces of plastic, the good life is only as far away as our next credit card purchase. Offers for credit cards show up in our mailboxes as often as junk mail. For those of you lucky ones who are already "preapproved," you need only sign the application and return it. But as a consumer advocate who has seen firsthand the damage which can be done to a family with credit cards, I wonder if these companies shouldn't be required to post warning labels on their cards as cigarette companies are required to do. I happened to read the fine print on a credit card application not long ago and saw that the issuer required that the applicant's total family income be at least $8000. Folks, if all you make is $8000 per year, the last thing you need is a credit card!

The economic uncertainties of recent years have contributed greatly to this worsening situation. The job losses which have been so prevalent in recent years have forced families to lose their homes, cars, and many other goods which they used credit to purchase. Many unemployed people have been pushed into using their credit cards to support themselves and their families for as long as their credit limits will allow. In no time they find themselves faced with $5000, $10,000, even $20,000 worth of debt on which they're paying as much as 21% per year in interest.

I also believe that a weakening of the moral and ethical fiber in many of America's citizens is a strong factor in the mass defaulting on debt. Too many people have jumped on the "buy-now-pay-later" bandwagon, and more than a few have done so with no intention of ever paying their creditors back. For these unscrupulous people, the only thing that matters is the satisfying of their needs and wants. To add insult to injury, we *all* foot the bill when debt becomes uncollectible, thanks to the government's policy of allowing credit grantors to take a tax deduction for this debt.

THE VALUE OF A GOOD CREDIT RECORD

Don't make the mistake of deciding that, because you don't buy anything with credit (if that's your situation), you don't need to worry about what your credit report looks like. More and more employers are running credit checks on prospective employees for the purpose of measuring their personal integrity. Even some property and casualty insurers (which includes auto insurance) are beginning to run credit checks on people whom they are contemplating insuring. In addition, I don't know how realistic it is to go through life presuming

CREDIT

you'll never have to buy anything on credit. Most people will probably need to use some form of credit to purchase homes, cars, and other high-dollar durable goods that lend themselves to being bought with credit. If you're one of those individuals who feels he doesn't need good credit because your spouse has it, remember that people die and couples get divorced. Don't be shortsighted about your need for a good credit record.

FREEDOM PRINCIPLE
Wisely used credit is a powerful
personal financial tool.

Credit itself is not bad; the *misuse* of credit is. In truth, credit allows you to buy assets you typically would be unable to. Take the purchase of a home, for example. As you may well know, a home represents not just a place for you and your family to live, but a sound investment and tax deduction as well. The interest you pay on the money you borrow to buy the home is generally much more than offset by the profit that you make when you sell the house after several years. If you don't sell the home, think of all the rent-free years you will enjoy living there, not to mention the equity that you can borrow against if the need arises. Home ownership is a good example of how you can borrow money to make money. Professional real estate investors operate on this basic principle to make fortunes.

If you have money to invest, buying shares of stock on margin is another way you can make strategic use of credit. When you use a margin account, the brokerage house is lending you money to buy additional shares you otherwise couldn't afford. Though I rarely recommend this strategy, in certain specific market conditions it can make sense. However, this should never be done with money you cannot afford to lose.

Another way you can use credit to positively impact your life is to use it to start a business. If you are eager to go into business for yourself and feel you have a surefire plan for success, you can use that plan to secure a loan from the bank. Most people don't have the financial resources required to start a business, so borrowing the money becomes somewhat of a requirement.

Even the credit card has its place in your financial tool chest, assuming you use it intelligently. For example, if you use your credit card to purchase a service of some kind, you can very often be excused from paying the bill if you found the service to be poor. It is the Truth-in-Lending Act which gives you this right. If you purchased a service which you found to be unsatisfactory, you should write a letter to the credit card issuer detailing the nature of your dissatisfaction. Send a copy of the letter to the merchant. Very often the issuer will simply remove the charge from your bill. You can also use credit cards strategically to give yourself an interest-free loan for about 50 days. Most Visa and MasterCard credit cards give the cardholder 25 grace days. So if you make your purchases right after the previous cycle's cutoff date for new purchases, you can have roughly 50 days to pay off those purchases without incurring a finance charge.

As you can see, credit can be a valuable resource if used wisely. Understanding the many strategies of using credit to build financial independence is an integral part of any serious financial plan.

KEEPING YOUR CREDIT REPORT ACCURATE

FREEDOM PRINCIPLE
Review a copy of your credit report once
each year to ensure good credit health.

A credit report is a record of your credit worthiness. Credit reporting agencies, or credit bureaus, serve as banks of information. This information comes from businesses and organizations all across the country who subscribe to the credit bureaus. The information pertains to your credit relationship with each of the businesses from which you have borrowed money. The bureaus assemble a profile on you which details your experiences in the world of credit, both good and bad. This profile is your credit report, and it will be accessed by any potential grantor of credit (as well as by some potential employers).

Because your credit report carries so much significance in daily life, you would do well to review it from time to time for accuracy. I suggest that you review it at least twice a year. Mistakes are common on credit reports, but you'll never know they exist until you check. Whenever I give a seminar, I like to ask how many audience members have ever found a mistake on their credit reports. Typically, the hands of about half the audience members shoot in the air. The three major credit reporting agencies are TRW, Equifax, and Trans Union. TRW will give you a free copy of your credit report once each year; Equifax and Trans Union will charge you $10 to $15. *Don't* simply get the free copy from TRW. You can't be sure which bureau a potential grantor of credit subscribes to. Play it safe and review all three. You can contact each of these major credit reporting agencies at the following locations:

TRW Information Services
505 City Parkway West
Orange, CA 92668
(714) 385-7500

Equifax Information Services
P.O. Box 740241
Atlanta, GA 30374-0241
(404) 885-8231

Trans Union
25249 Country Club Boulevard
North Olmstead, OH 44070
(312) 258-1717

FREEDOM PRINCIPLE
Dispute inaccurate information in
your credit report and demand that
it be removed.

I've heard people say that there's nothing that can be done about incorrect information contained on a credit report. That notion is completely false. The Fair Credit Reporting Act, which is your legal protection from the malicious or negligent behavior of creditors and credit bureaus (as far as your credit record is concerned), gives you the right to challenge these entities on a number of issues.

If you notice incorrect information on your credit report, use the following procedure: Write a letter of dispute which informs the credit reporting agency about the complete nature of the error. You will want to list the name of the creditor in question, the code indicated (the type of these will vary from bureau to bureau), the account number accorded to the debt listed, and a brief description of the inaccurate data. Be sure to take this up matter with the *credit reporting agency*, not the creditor. It is the bureau's records which reflect the inaccuracy, and it is only their records which will be reviewed by other grantors of credit.

Once the bureau receives your letter, *they* will contact the creditor for verification of the item. The credit bureau has a "reasonable" period of time to take the matter up with the creditor and get back with you with the results of their investigation. The "reasonable" period has since been defined as 30 days. If the creditor admits that the entry is indeed an error, or simply doesn't report back to the bureau within the allotted time, the item should be removed immediately by the bureau. You will find a sample letter for this particular type of dispute located in Appendix B at the back of this book.

FREEDOM PRINCIPLE
Don't try to correct inaccurate information through the original creditor or collection agency.

Not knowing any better, when many people find a piece of incorrect information contained in their credit reports, they believe the proper way of handling the situation is with the creditor directly. After all, they reason, it is this creditor who posted the information, so it must be his records which need correcting. Not true.

First of all, the credit reporting agencies can be every bit as responsible for the posting of inaccurate data as the creditors are. Very often the information received by the agencies in these cases is accurate, but it belongs in someone else's record, not yours. Also, remember that a creditor is a business that is in business to make money. It doesn't want to bother wasting time (in their opinion) and money seeking to correct what is to them a small administrative error. Finally, it is not the creditor that is covered by the Fair Credit Reporting Act. Rather, it is the credit bureau. If you want to keep the law on your side as much as possible in this endeavor, which I wholeheartedly recommend that you do for best results, take the matter up with the credit agency/bureau.

FREEDOM PRINCIPLE
Demand that negative information which is over seven years old be removed from your credit report.

A common question I get from listeners of my radio show is "How long does bad information stay on my credit report?"

Well, it depends on what exactly you mean by "bad information." According to the Fair Credit Reporting Act, negative information in general may not remain on the report for longer than seven years from the date it was originally posted. There is an exception to this, however. Bankruptcies may remain on the report for up to ten years. If this were a more perfect world, you could rely on the credit bureau to automatically delete the information from your report in accordance with the time constraints outlined in the Act. But I don't take it for granted that the bureau will remove this information from my report when they're supposed to, and neither should you. Here again, the power of the pen (as well as the Fair Credit Reporting Act) is on your side.

The procedure you should follow is to write a letter to the credit bureau which states that you would like to see information removed from your report because it exists past the time allowed by the Fair Credit Reporting Act. In this letter you will want to include the name of the creditor, the code, and the account number. You will find a sample letter for expressing this grievance in Appendix B.

FREEDOM PRINCIPLE
**Dispute information on your credit report
which is accurate but negative, in order
that it may be removed.**

The dispute method of removing negative items from a credit report is used effectively by many people to remove inaccurate or dated information. Did you know, however, that it can also be used to remove information which is accurate? That may be different from what you've heard before. Financial counselors who discuss this general subject typically say that there is nothing you can do to remove information which is both accurate and within the seven-year time limit.

CREDIT

CREDIT

Well, there is something you can do, and the mechanism which permits this can be found in the wording of a particular section in the Fair Credit Reporting Act.

First, let me say that I would never advise you to implement a strategy which is illegal, immoral, or unethical. I say this because some who hear that the removal of this information can be accomplished assume that there is something not quite right about doing it. But that is not true. Section 605 of the Fair Credit Reporting Act says, in effect, that negative information can remain on a credit report for *as long as* seven and ten years (ten for bankruptcies); it does not say that the data *must* remain on the report for seven and ten years. The specific wording reads as follows:

> . . . no consumer reporting agency may make any consumer report containing any of the following items of information:
>
> 1. Cases under Title II of the United States Code or under the Bankruptcy Act that, from the date of the entry of the order for relief or the date of adjudication, as the case may be, antedate the report by more than ten years.
>
> 2. Suits and judgments which, from date of entry, antedate the report by more then seven years or until the governing statute of limitations has expired, whichever is the longer period.

You need to be careful about how you construct your letter to the credit bureau, because you don't want to make any claims which are untrue. You can't, for example, ask the bureau to investigate the information on the basis you believe it to be inaccurate if you know full well that it's not. Specifically, you should list the details of the entry in your letter as you did in the letter which requests the removal of inaccurate information, but with a difference. In *this* letter, simply ask the credit bureau to "reinvestigate" or "reverify" the data. The credit bureau will go through the same procedures it uses to recheck inaccurate information, contacting the creditor, and reporting back to you within 30 days.

Now I know you must be wondering how well this really works. After all, does not the creditor simply have to do a quick check of its records, see that the information is correct, and report back to the credit bureau accordingly? Well, that's true, and that happens frequently. However, what *also* happens frequently is that the creditor, who doesn't want to be bothered investigating the legitimacy of an old debt (remember what I said about the creditor's concern with making money), simply neglects to report back to the credit bureau within the 30-day time limit. At that point the credit bureau is required to delete the information. I'll tell you in advance that for this strategy to be effective, you'll have to be persistent. If the credit bureau reports back to you that the information has been reverified, simply write another letter requesting that they investigate it *again*. It may take you two or three series of letter-writings to make a significant improvement in your credit record, but that kind of effort is worth the result.

Two more things. First, bankruptcies are very difficult to remove in this way. The nature of bankruptcies, including the meticulous record-keeping which follows them, simply doesn't allow for their removal from credit reports in this fashion. Having said that, I will also tell you that it *has been done*; however, don't be surprised if your efforts don't bear much fruit. Also, it is very difficult to remove negative information related to a credit card account which is still active. Your answer is to either pay off the balance or transfer it to a new card. After the balance is zeroed out, close the account and begin your dispute procedures. For your convenience, I have included a sample letter for initiating this particular dispute process in Appendix B.

CREDIT

FREEDOM PRINCIPLE
Send a follow-up letter to the credit
bureau if you don't hear back on your
initial dispute letter within 30 days.

The Fair Credit Reporting Act requires that disputed
information be either reverified within a reasonable period
of time (30 days) or removed. What do you do, though, if
you haven't heard back from the credit bureau, and it has
been 40, 50, or 60 days? You should send a follow-up letter
to the credit bureau. This letter should be polite but quite
firm, indicating that you are still awaiting an answer and
once again citing the Fair Credit Reporting Act. A sample
copy of a follow-up letter is contained in Appendix B.

FREEDOM PRINCIPLE
Demand that unauthorized
credit inquiries be removed from
your credit report.

Typically found at the end of a credit report is the
"Inquiries" section. An inquiry means that the listed company
or organization has seen a copy of your credit report; inquiry
records are maintained for two years, although there is no
statute of limitations for credit inquiries as there is for negative information. Wherever you apply for credit, the company
to whom you're applying will show up on your report under
the "Inquiries" section.

You should be aware that potential grantors of credit shy
away from applicants who have excessive inquiries listed. It is
presumed that anyone who seeks to take on a lot of debt may be
irresponsible and thus potentially less likely to honor his or her
commitments. That's why it is so important that you seek to have
unauthorized credit inquiries removed from your report. An
unauthorized inquiry is one which has apparently been made by

a business that did not receive permission from you to review a copy of your credit report. As with the disputing of inaccurate information, don't waste your time taking the matter up with the inquiring party. There's a good chance the data was incorrectly placed on your report by the bureau anyway. Simply write a letter to the credit bureau requesting that the unauthorized inquiries be removed immediately. For assistance, refer to Appendix B to find a sample letter used for unauthorized inquiry removal.

FREEDOM PRINCIPLE
Add positive information about your credit history to your file at the credit bureau.

It is much more likely for untrue negative information to show up on your credit report than it is for positive information. If upon reviewing your credit report you notice that it contains no information about a credit card account you have been faithfully paying on, or nowhere mentions the auto loan obligation you have been meeting every month, then it's time to ask the bureau to include this favorable information about your history in their files. My suggestion would be for you to make copies of all relevant paperwork concerning this missing account, and send it along with the letter detailing the request. You may also want to include the name of the loan officer who handles your account.

FREEDOM PRINCIPLE
Contact the Federal Trade Commission (FTC) if the credit bureau is uncooperative in correcting your file.

The Federal Trade Commission is a governmental body which oversees credit practices and serves as the policing authority for most credit-related matters. Among the many laws they are charged with enforcing is the Fair Credit Reporting Act. If you have a complaint about a credit bureau which may not be conducting itself in accordance with the provisions of the Act, simply write a letter to the FTC registering your grievance.

If, for example, you are having a difficult time extracting information about the status of your dispute over inaccurate information, you may want to indicate in your next follow-up letter to the bureau that if you don't hear from them immediately, you will lodge an official complaint with the Federal Trade Commission. If that course of action brings no results, then I would advise you to write a detailed letter to the FTC which relates all that has transpired up to this point. By the way, by contacting the FTC at 202-326-3650, you can request a free brochure on the Fair Credit Reporting Act.

FREEDOM PRINCIPLE
Demand a free copy of your credit report
after a potential grantor has denied
your application for credit.

If you apply for credit and are denied, the organization or business to which you applied may not simply inform you of the denial and leave it at that. If the denial was based in whole or in part on information contained in your credit report, the business has an obligation, per the Fair Credit Reporting Act, to provide you with the name and address of the credit bureau which was accessed. Furthermore, you are entitled to receive a free copy of your credit report whenever you are denied credit on the basis of any information contained in the report. This entitlement also exists because of the Fair Credit Reporting Act, and the request should be made in writing to the grantor who denied the application.

FREEDOM PRINCIPLE
Beware of credit repair companies that guarantee you a clean credit record.

All of the focus on clean credit and credit rights over the past few years has spawned a new type of business: professional credit repair. These credit repair clinics work to clean the blemishes off your credit report. First, I'll give you my take on these sorts of operations, and then I'll say something which will surely surprise you.

Many credit repair clinics will guarantee that they can give you a squeaky-clean credit record. However, unless they are prepared to use illegal or unethical means to achieve their results, this is very difficult to achieve. Unfortunately, many such companies *do* engage in this kind of behavior. One of the methods used involves stealing good credit records and selling them to people who have poor credit records.[2] To do this, the company will typically have someone working for them who is either an employee of a credit agency or who is otherwise able to tap into the file base. As desperate as you may be for good credit, be very careful. It is quite illegal to do much of what these "sure thing" credit repair clinics are recommending, and you may get much more (not all good) than you bargained for when you sign on with one of these companies and pay their high fees.

As mentioned in the beginning of this chapter, I have my own credit repair service, "The Credit Doctor." There are some key differences, however, between the kinds of services I just spoke about and the type of service I offer. First, my fees are a lot lower. One reason they are lower is because I don't need to charge for the risk I'm taking or the hassle I'm going through in setting up a whole new credit identity for you, simply because I don't do that. My service, and other services like it, work within the law to clean up your credit record by persistently using the industry-accepted methods.

CREDIT

Actually, I've outlined the basics of many of the methods in this chapter already, and that's another important point: The legally run and ethically minded credit repair services don't do anything more than what you can do for yourself. They simply do it for you if you don't have the time or the inclination to do it on your own. Finally, these above-board services don't guarantee to give you perfect credit or that they can remove a bankruptcy from your record. The only thing they may guarantee is that they will work diligently to improve the appearance of your credit record as much as possible.

Remember, do your homework before signing on with a credit repair clinic. You may have some responsibility if you allow an unscrupulous credit repair service to repair your credit through the use of illegal means. If you would like more information on the service I provide, call 1-800-877-2022 and ask to speak with The Credit Doctor.

FREEDOM PRINCIPLE
Get a secured credit card to help
reestablish your good credit record.

The last subject I would like to discuss in this chapter is secured credit cards. I mention secured credit cards in Chapter 4, when talking about how a person with no credit record (to speak of) can go about initiating at least some kind of favorable history. Even though "no credit history" usually means no information good or bad, many banks are leery about issuing unsecured Visas or MasterCards to individuals with no payment history.

Let's go over what a secured card is, just to be sure you know. A secured credit card is one which the cardholder obtains in exchange for depositing a sum of money with the issuer. The credit limit awarded to the cardholder is usually equal to the amount of his deposit. If the cardholder deposits $1000 in the issuing bank, the bank will provide a $1000 credit limit on the card.

This, of course, is much different from how the more common unsecured credit cards work. With unsecured cards, your card is issued without your having to put any money at all into the issuing bank. It is simply your creditworthiness and your promise to pay that the issuing bank relies on. You can see that with a secured card, the issuing bank is not assuming much risk. That's why getting approved for one is basically a guaranteed thing.

A secured credit card does not look any different from any other type of Visa or MasterCard. Many people are reluctant to pursue this option for fear that there is some mark on the card which signals the merchant that it's secured; I guess they are afraid of being stigmatized. The fact is, no one other than you knows that the card is secured.

Now that you know what a secured card is, you should be able to clearly see how it can be a tremendous benefit to someone with a checkered credit past. The secured card affords this person the opportunity to reenter the credit world and begin to establish a record for making payments reliably. It would help the perception of your creditworthiness tremendously if you could combine the record of your wisely used secured card with the cleaning up of your existing credit record. You will find a list of secured cards contained in Appendix A.

START NOW

Although I don't believe that credit reporting agencies intentionally deal in bad faith, you should be aware of how costly their honest mistakes can be, and what you can do about them.

CREDIT

While it is true that repairing your credit record will require work on your part, the price of not doing it could be a life of financial agony.

There is really no good reason why you should not obtain and keep good credit. Think about good credit as the jumper cables you keep in the trunk of your car that you hope you may never need. Good credit can be a valuable source of protection that you may someday need very urgently.

CREDIT

6

SCHEMES
AND SCAMS

One morning I received a phone call from my Florida office. The vice president of my Financial Planning Division informed me that one of our clients was going to close her account and put her money in a tax-free investment. My curiosity was piqued, and I asked the vice president what kind of tax-free investment—municipal bonds, perhaps? He answered no and went on to explain that our client had recently attended a seminar and was told that if she set up a certain kind of trust there would never be any tax liability to either her or the trust.

Neither I nor any of my associates had ever heard of such a concept, so I checked with several friends of mine who are attorneys to see if maybe I was missing something. All of them said the same thing: There was no such thing as a tax-free trust. We called the client back immediately and informed her that her money was on the way and also what we had found out through our research. But her position was unshakable. She was bound and determined to turn over her money to the person she had seen at a seminar. This is despite the fact that both I and my associates explained to her that she was being deceived, and also that we had confirmed our belief with several attorneys.

This chapter is about "Schemes and Scams," and as P. T. Barnum was once quoted as saying, "There is a sucker born every minute." As controversial as it may sound, I believe that most of us are victims of our own handiwork. If it were not for the greed that many of us are motivated by, we would probably use more of our common sense. The idea that we can get rich quick in America or not pay taxes or even lose weight while we sleep may sound good, but it just isn't true. The foundation of success for con artists is finding a person whose greed has clouded his common sense. The Postal Service has said for years that "if it sounds too good to be true, it probably is." This chapter will serve as a self-defense manual against the most commonly perpetrated schemes and scams going on in America today.

Whether you call it a scheme or a scam, a flim or a flam, fraud by any other name is still fraud. The widespread use of fraud to fleece people of their hard-earned cash proves that America's greatest asset—freedom—can be used successfully by certain unscrupulous citizens to destroy the dreams and bank accounts of other citizens. In that regard, freedom is a double-edged sword: If you want to see government stay off your back and not bury you further under a pile of regulations, you're going to have to do your part: Don't allow yourself to become victimized by people and organizations who clearly can't deliver on what they promise.

Although I am gravely concerned about the fraud I see daily that masks itself as legitimate enterprise, I can't help but wonder about the mindset of some of the people who fall victim to this stuff. I'm very concerned that we are fast approaching a time in which many government laws will exist simply to protect us from ourselves. Let me make this point very clear: Anyone who is clearly guilty of using deception or trickery to separate people from their money should be punished to the fullest extent of whatever laws are available which cover that sort of activity. I do believe, though, that if more people simply listened to their good common sense, these schemers and scammers would have to do some honest work for a change.

Perpetrators of fraud-for-profit achieve success by exploiting one of the following four characteristics of the human condition: greed, fear, generosity, or hope. For most of these scams to work, people have to be willing to believe that the unbelievable is true. They have to engage, at least temporarily, in a suspension of their disbelief. This is especially true of the people who are motivated by greed, because some of these greed-based scams should appear clearly ridiculous to anyone. This is a good illustration of just how powerful money's influence can be, luring people into behaviors they wouldn't otherwise engage in and successfully convincing them to ignore their common sense. Ultimately, though, money cannot be blamed. It is not said in the Bible that money is the root of all evil; it is said that the *love* of money is the root of all evil (1 Timothy 6:10). Love of money is a weakness, and like all weaknesses, it can only be repelled by perspective, focus, and discipline.

I believe it is irresponsible for media organizations to allow perpetrators of fraud to buy advertising time and space so they may make their pitches. The response "We're not responsible for the actions of those who buy time on our station" is really pretty lame, and in fact some outlets are beginning to find that they are being regarded more and more as having a degree of responsibility for the behavior of these hucksters. The fact that something is technically legal does not mean that it is ethical. That is the difference between adhering to the letter of the law and adhering to the spirit of the law. Wouldn't it be nice if more people did their part to help shore up this nation's spirit and spirituality?

GREED-BASED SCAMS

Greed-based scams are probably the type that get the most attention from the media. These scams typically cause the greatest financial loss because they are usually financially based. Generally the theme involves an easy way to get your hands on a substantial amount of money by doing little in return. Such cons as large loans for people with bad credit or business opportunities that provide a "no effort" big payoff top the list. The fact is that greed-based scams are probably the most successful of all types of scams. Although these tactics can usually be spotted a mile away, the person filled with greed chooses to believe them anyway. I cannot tell you the number of times I have broken out in laughter when one of these scams was explained to me by my staff. I find it hard to comprehend that people are really buying into these so-called moneymaking opportunities. Yet we all have greed to some extent, and if left uncontrolled it can give a scam artist just what he is looking for.

FREEDOM PRINCIPLE
Learn to recognize the
work-at-home scam.

The work-at-home scam comes in many different forms. Basically, the scam's pitch is that you can make a fortune working out of your home doing fairly simple tasks, tasks which may take only "minutes a day." Perhaps the most famous of all of these is the envelope-stuffing scam. You've probably seen the ads: "Make $1000 a week processing mail" or "Make $1000 a week stuffing envelopes." The ad goes on to ask you to send a self-addressed, stamped envelope to some post office box. Once you send your envelope, the scammer returns a letter to you which describes in very general terms how the program works. At the end of the letter there will be a request for a $25 setup fee to get you going. If you think envelope-stuffing is the way to go, you will send in your $25, only to get a letter back which says the way to make all that money is by placing in *your* newspaper the same ad that *you* answered.

This scam is a good example of what I was talking about when I referred to "suspension of disbelief." Does anyone really believe that he can make over $50,000 a year stuffing envelopes? Other home-based employment scams are constructed very similarly. The notions proposed in each of the ads are ludicrous, but if that fact doesn't tip you off that there's a problem, nothing will.

FREEDOM PRINCIPLE
Beware of the advance-fee-loan scam.

The advance-fee-loan scam proposes that you can get a loan of $50,000 to $100,000 even if your credit history is poor. Although the ads for this scam are typically found in the backs of America's many tabloid newspapers and magazines, I actually saw one posted to a telephone pole while I was stopped at a red light not long ago. The ads usually read something like this: "Need money? Find out how you can get a loan up to $100,000. Bad credit, no credit, no problem. Call 555-1234." When you call the number, you will usually get a recording which will tell you to send $20 to some post office box. The $20 is billed as an application fee. Once the scammer gets your money, he *may* send you an application for the loan. Even if he does, you two will never have contact after that.

The Federal Trade Commission is hot on the trail of the advance-fee-loan scammers, so if you've been victimized, you may want to contact the Commission. You can find the address in Appendix D.

FREEDOM PRINCIPLE
Don't let yourself be fooled by
the lottery scam.

The scams just get better and better, although I must question the good sense of anyone who allows himself to be taken in by this one. The lottery scam works like this: A desperate-looking stranger approaches a person on the street and claims to hold a winning lottery ticket. The stranger, usually someone of foreign appearance, tells the person he is unable to collect his winning because he is in this country illegally and has no Social Security number, and is therefore ineligible to legitimately win the contest.

The stranger then goes on to ask the person if he would do him the favor of a lifetime and collect the prize for him. If the person agrees to do it, the stranger gives him the ticket, but not before requesting and getting a "security deposit" of sorts for the ticket. "After all," says the stranger, "I can't really be expected to hand over a million-dollar ticket without at least some insurance that you'll return." This makes good sense to the unwitting victim, who will fork over, say, $1000 to the stranger. Once that transaction has taken place, the stranger disappears with the $1000, and the victim gets to keep a perfectly useless lottery ticket. This scam works especially well between two people of the same ethnicity, as the perpetrator can successfully play on the sympathies of the victim with respect to his citizenship status.

FREEDOM PRINCIPLE
It's "let the buyer beware" when you
order anything by mail.

It is a serious federal offense for anyone to use the mail system to defraud consumers, but that doesn't seem to hurt business in this area of "scamworld" very much. Much of what is sold through the mail is junk, but these scammers are pretty smart, because they will send you something for your money, even if it's useless. It's not like they take your money and leave you with nothing. Because you actually did receive something for your money, you'll be less likely to complain and more likely to chalk up the experience to living and learning.

Let's say, for example, that you buy some type of skin lotion. What you get for your money may be nothing more than white goo, but as long as it doesn't dissolve your skin, you probably won't care that much. The fact remains, though, that you *did* get ripped off. Guarding against these kinds of scams is more difficult, because it is impossible to know the legitimate offers from the illegitimate ones simply by flipping through a magazine. My suggestion to you is simply not to make any of these kinds of purchases unless you know the company to be legitimate, either by name recognition or from a personal reference. If you choose to take your chances with an unknown entity, then that's exactly what you'll be doing.

FEAR-BASED SCAMS

The scams which play off the fears of people may be the saddest of all, since fear is one of the few reasonable justifications I can think of for suspending one's disbelief. The fear-based frauds I'll be talking about in this chapter are aimed exclusively at the elderly, which makes the whole thing even more disgusting. In some countries (such as Japan) the elderly are revered for their experience and wisdom, but in the United States the elderly are frequently regarded as targets to be easily abused and defrauded. The way our senior citizens are treated by scammers speaks volumes about the weakening of this nation's moral fiber.

FREEDOM PRINCIPLE
Don't buy life insurance policies designed
only for the elderly.

I talk about this subject somewhat in the chapter on retirement planning, but I also include it in this chapter because of the deception involved.

According to the television ads which pitch this type of insurance, any older American who fears he doesn't have enough insurance to help out his spouse is in luck. Why? Well, now that person can buy additional coverage for just 50 cents per day. These policies are typically advertised as requiring no medical exam and even guaranteeing approval. How in the world can any insurance company afford to do this?

They can afford to do it in basically one of two ways. First, the amount of insurance coverage is so low that it wouldn't be cost-effective for the insurance company to bother paying for a physical for you or to worry about excluding you from coverage; the high premiums charged (relative to the amount of coverage received) more than pay for any risks that "guaranteed approval" would incur.

The second tactic is to make the total cost of the insurance coverage appear cheaper than it actually is. This is done by selling the insurance in units of coverage. One unit is equal to X number of dollars in a death benefit. So, even though one unit may cost *only* $10 per month, you may need to purchase five or six units to get coverage of, say, $2000. This means you would end up paying $50 to $60 a month (or about $600 per year) for $2000 of coverage. Although the company will tell you that the amount of coverage offered by a unit *does* typically go up in each successive year, be aware that it does not go up fast enough to keep up with the outrageous premiums you're paying.

The deception here lies in the fact that nowhere in the advertising does it say how much coverage you're actually getting or what it is costing. These ads are great examples of how things which are not true are nevertheless implied.

Another variation is the life insurance geared specifically toward veterans of the U.S. armed forces. The basic claim made is that the insurance is offered at low cost to veterans, and that it is out of deference to some special tie-in with the U.S. government. Actually, the ads don't come out and *say* that the government has anything to do with the insurance, but that message is clearly implied. But the fact is that there is no life insurance plan for veterans which is either directly or indirectly sponsored by the U.S. government. Additionally, this insurance is very expensive, and coverage is not guaranteed to all veterans, although the ads clearly imply that it is. More deception.

FREEDOM PRINCIPLE
Examine any prospective Medigap insurance coverage purchases with a very careful, even cynical, eye.

You've heard the line: "Pick up where Medicare leaves off." I have just one question: Where exactly does Medicare leave off?

The fact is that Medicare provides significant health insurance benefits, especially if you subscribe to Part B coverage in addition to Part A coverage. While it is true that you are responsible for paying the deductibles as well as for making (if necessary) a 20% co-insurance payment which is present in *some* features of the coverage, you should carefully evaluate your ability to meet these costs on your own *before* purchasing expensive Medigap coverage. Many of the ads which push Medigap coverage try to play on the fears of consumers by implying that Medicare covers only a limited portion of health care expenses. While technically that *can* be true, depending on your particular situation, the limit is a lot closer to 100% than they might otherwise lead you to believe.

Be forewarned that if you decide to answer an advertisement for a Medigap supplemental policy, you will undoubtedly find yourself wrestling with a salesman sooner or later. These agents use high-pressure sales tactics in an effort to get you to purchase a lot more coverage than you really need. Because there are many different types of Medigap coverage available, many unscrupulous salesmen will bank on your confusion and uncertainty to see that they are able to sell you as much insurance as possible. To guard against this potential eventuality, I would suggest that you contact the United Seniors Health Cooperative at 202-393-6022 if you have any questions. This organization is dedicated to assisting senior citizens with their health care needs, and can provide a wealth of information (for a nominal charge) on Medicare and Medigap coverages.

GENEROSITY-BASED SCAMS

The scams which take advantage of a person's generosity and charitable inclinations are also pretty sick. Who doesn't, at one time or another, want to do something to help the less fortunate? Who in his right mind would think there is something strange or unethical about trying to help blind children, mentally handicapped children, or other unfortunates? I do want to say that, after reading this chapter, I hope you won't feel any differently about donating time and/or money to help those who are truly in need. I only want to help you refine your ability to spot the wolves in sheep's clothing.

FREEDOM PRINCIPLE
Don't be taken in by the "I will
work for food" scam.

I know you've all seen them: The wretched-looking individuals who stand on street corners and hold up signs which read "I will work for food." Almost 100% of the time, though, the individuals are scamming you, because they don't have any *intention* of working for food or anything else. The scam can be quite effective for the following reason: Unlike a typical panhandler, the "I will work for food" person is proclaiming that he doesn't *want* a hand out—just an opportunity to work so he can provide himself with the barest of essentials. Because we feel greater sympathy for someone who so obviously wants to work for his livelihood, but is unable to do anything about it, many of us will just give the poor unfortunate a dollar or two to help him get by while he waits for someone who will employ him.

Do *not* be taken in by this scam. If you don't believe it is a scam, just do what one of my employees did: Tell the person that if he comes with you, you'll put him to work doing chores and other odd jobs, and that he'll be rewarded with, say, a bag of groceries. The response will probably be similar to the one my employee received: "Uh, no thanks. Can you just give me a buck or something?" The fact is that this scam works so well that the person would be *crazy* to leave his perch and go off to work several hours for a bag of groceries. Law enforcement officials say that some of these people, working the right "territory," can make over $500 a week. Some of the more unscrupulous scammers will even have their children stand out there with them, playing further on your sympathies.

Actually, anyone who is that desperate to work can find a job. Many cities, both large and small, have jobs available through temporary-service agencies. With these, anyone who wants to work simply shows up in the morning and is taken with other laborers to a job site of one type or another. Typically, the work is basic manual labor. At the end of the day the workers are returned to the job center or temporary-service agency, where they are paid.

Again, in no way am I asking that you ignore your charitable inclinations. Giving to those less fortunate, whether it's time or money, is a decent, honorable, and spiritually satisfying endeavor. You want to be sure, however, that you're giving to those who are truly in need.

FREEDOM PRINCIPLE
Don't be taken in by the charity box or
vending machine scam.

Very often, when you go into a restaurant or some other business premises, you will find a charity box or vending machine posted there. I'm sure you've seen them: the countertop cardboard stands which dispense candy and ask for an honor donation in return. The box indicates that the proceeds will go to whatever charity has its name splashed all over the box. Most people who contribute feel good about the fact that their donation will benefit people less fortunate than themselves.

But how much of that money do you think actually goes to the advertised charity? 100%? 80%? 50%? How does 0% strike you? Perhaps I need to explain to you how this scam works. First, an enterprising small businessman will get his hands on a bunch of these honor boxes and the products that go in them, which is very easy to do. Then this person will contact a charity and make a contractual agreement with them, an agreement which basically says that he can use the name of the charity on his boxes in exchange for a fee. The fee normally runs about $2.00 per month per box. So if this person sets up 50 boxes, he is obligated to pay the charity $100 per month. Typically, 10% of the proceeds go to the merchant in exchange for the use of his location. The rest goes into the pocket of our enterprising young friend. Actually, then, the charity *is* realizing some benefit from the proceeds; where do you think the $100 a month comes from?

This is a good example of a scam which is not illegal, but is quite unethical. A better way to contribute to these charities is to do so directly, removing from the equation any middlemen who exist only to make a profit. I realize the competition for charitable dollars is quite fierce, and that there are an innumerable number of worthwhile charities out there, but I have to wonder about the integrity of any charitable organization which would be a party to such deception. As a matter of fact, it should come as little surprise to you that many of these organizations are under investigation, based on accusations that only a very small amount of what they take in is actually spent on the stated charitable purpose.

HOPE-BASED SCAMS

Finally, there are the scams which attempt to take advantage of your hopefulness—your hope for a better life, your hope for obtaining and keeping your own home, your hope for business success. These scams may not be as morally bankrupt as some of the others, but that may be like arguing that someone who murders one person isn't as bad as someone who murders two people.

FREEDOM PRINCIPLE
Hold on to your credit card when responding to a "You are a Winner!" mailer.

Have you ever actually responded to one of those by-mail notifications which informs you that "you have definitely been awarded one of the following five prizes," and proceeds to list four great things and one cheap piece of garbage? Do you really have any doubt as to which prize is actually going to be awarded to you?

These scams basically work one of two ways. One way is that for you to claim your prize, you must dial a "900" number which costs you, say, $3.00 per minute. After you're put on hold and passed around from representative to representative, you've been on the phone 10 to 15 minutes by the time the "verification process" is complete. You will receive a nice prize worth all of about $5.00, and meanwhile will have paid out $45.00 to the company for responding.

The other, and more dangerous, way this scam works is that in order to receive your prize, you're asked to charge a fee of a few hundred dollars on your credit card to defray the cost of contest "marketing expenses." In fact, the only reason you received this notification in the first place is because you have a credit card, which companies can easily determine from certain types of mailing lists. With these contests, the prize you receive might be a little nicer (say, a $50 gift certificate of some kind), but come on—you've just paid $200 or $300 to get it! I know everybody likes to be a winner, but please use your common sense and read the fine print on the "winner's certificate" before you respond.

FREEDOM PRINCIPLE
Beware of unscrupulous credit repair clinics.

I talk briefly about this in the chapter on credit repair, but I want you to understand very clearly about how the unscrupulous credit repair companies work and how dangerous they can be to you.

The type of clinic I'm referring to is *not* the type which works to repair credit within legal, industry-accepted means. The ones I'm referring to here will risk just about anything to deliver on their outrageous guarantees of 100% clean credit or total removal of a bankruptcy. If you're in a desperate credit situation, it's understandable that you would find these claims to be quite a temptation. Don't give in. First, you will pay an exorbitant fee for the service, as high as $1000. Second, the "service" involves credit bureau insiders or professional computer hackers tapping into credit records and switching over an unsuspecting person's clean file with that of the customer's. These services will also make good on their promises by creating a whole new identity for you.

Everything these particular types of credit repair services do is unethical, and much of it is illegal. You can very easily find yourself on the wrong side of the law, and even facing penalties if it can be proven that you had at least a hint of what was going on.

FREEDOM PRINCIPLE
Hungry home buyers, watch out for the "trap mortgage."

The "trap mortgage" isn't really a scam per se, but it definitely qualifies as being unethical. The trap mortgage works like this: Let's say you are a potential home buyer who has found your dream house, but you can't get approved for a mortgage from a typical lender. Desperate, you turn to finance companies for hope, and you find one which will give you a mortgage, but at a rate far above the going interest rate at the time. You really want the house, so you take the deal.

What commonly happens next is that not long after you are in your dream house, you begin to fall behind on the payments (which you should never have agreed to in the first place). Before long you are foreclosed upon and the finance company now owns your house.

What makes this practice unethical is that any professional who works in the lending business knows that there is a generally accepted standard for determining how much of what you make should be paid out as mortgage payments. That standard is no more than 30% of your total gross income. With a trap mortgage, families typically commit 40% to 50% of their annual income to the year's worth of payments. All these companies have to do is play on your desire for the home, and they've got you. The key, then, is to listen to your good sense; don't obligate yourself to payments you know will be difficult to make.

FREEDOM PRINCIPLE
Watch out for companies which take advantage of your dreams to become the next Thomas Edison.

So you think you have a great idea for a product. Perhaps you envision this product lining the shelves of department stores all across the country, and you picture consumers coming from great distances to buy it. Whoa, slow down. All you have at this point is an idea. Where do you go from here?

Well, one place you *shouldn't* go is to companies which, for a fee, say they will develop and market the product you have thought up. Actually, what they do first is ask you to send in your idea to see if they like it. You are thrilled, of course, when "after careful evaluation" this company determines that you have come up with a winner. The euphoria you feel over the potential of becoming one of America's newest multi-millionaires allows you to find it perfectly understandable when the company says it must charge you a $500 fee to defray the initial expenses associated with getting started. But $500 and a few months later, all you have to show for the experience is a few sketches of your vision and a sample letter you can use to approach potential manufacturers with.

What I have shown you here is just a sample of the many schemes and scams which are thrust on the American people every day. If you believe you have been ripped off, I suggest that you contact the office of the Attorney General in your state. I also suggest contacting the Federal Trade Commission, as well as the Postal Inspector if you were defrauded through the mails. The addresses for many appropriate complaint contacts can be found in Appendix D.

I would also encourage you to demand satisfaction from the media source of the advertising you initially responded to. If you saw the ad on a local television station, I would hound them for a refund. If you saw it in a magazine, I would hound *them* for a refund. You will probably find that many of these media sources will stick to their "we're not responsible . . ." story, but if you become somewhat of a thorn in their side, you may at least get the privilege of being the person responsible for seeing that these irresponsible advertisers get kicked off the air.

Finally, I want to say something about the Better Business Bureau. The Better Business Bureau is frequently regarded as being the savior of the consumer. But really, the Better Business Bureau is, for all intents and purposes, pretty useless. They are not a regulatory agency, and in fact they possess no kinds of regulatory powers at all. Once you have been defrauded, there is nothing this group can do for you. You *can* use the Bureau to determine if a company you're considering transacting business with has had any complaints lodged against it in the past, but because the vast majority of ripped-off consumers simply take their beatings quietly, without saying a word, this tactic may be of limited value. This is especially true when you consider that the Bureau only tracks complaints made to them, and doesn't account for complaints made to other agencies (such as the Attorney General's office).

Private businesses have the freedom to do business with you, and you have the freedom to do business with them. You also have the freedom *not* to do business with them. Freedom is the key here, but as with any freedom, you need to use it *responsibly*. In this case the responsibility is to yourself. Use the resources of wisdom and good sense which God has blessed you with, and you should be able to steer clear of these kinds of troubles.

7

How to
Buy a Car

In 1981 I had the thrill of buying my first car. I had just turned 16 and received a driver's license, which at the time I believed to have been my greatest life accomplishment. My first car was a 1965 Chevrolet. My dad and I negotiated with the owner and felt we got a bargain at $125. The car was not much to speak of, but it did run, and I proudly drove it home and parked it in our driveway, to the dismay of our neighbors, who saw it as nothing but a bucket of rust.

After I got out of college, I decided it was time to buy a new car. The idea was very intimidating, to say the least: a monthly payment, plus insurance, plus what if someone stole it? Growing up on the South Side of Chicago, I learned there were many traditions unique to Midwestern natives, and this was true with car buying as well. The way Midwesterners approach car-buying is similar to hunting: All the men in the family, as many generations back as you can muster, go to the dealer together. This means if grandson wants to buy a car, then father and grandfather (and, if he is still alive, great-grandfather) all go to the dealer together to use their collective manliness to try to intimidate the dealer into giving them the best possible deal.

I have subsequently learned that there is a better way to buy a car, and you don't need anyone to go with you. You can show up on your own, and you can even do it over the phone if you wish. In this chapter you will learn the basic common-sense approach to car-buying that I was taught by several former car dealership salespeople who have appeared on my radio broadcasts as frequent guests.

I wish cars didn't look so good and weren't so much fun to drive, because they are *such* a poor investment of one's money. Car manufacturers seem to have our number, however, because rarely does a day go by when I don't find myself turning my head for a better look at some new, shiny model which has just motored past me. The fact is that cars are being constructed in sportier styles than ever before. Economy cars and luxury cars, heretofore never coming close to being confused with sports cars, are now coming off the assembly lines with rear spoilers, sport wheelcovers, and a sleek, low-to-the-ground appearance, which can let just about anyone pretend that he is a participant in the Grand Prix of Monaco. There just aren't many ugly cars being made anymore, and that fact alone is making an already auto-obsessed society even more fanatic.

The other problem we face in trying to be "car-resistant" is that our society seems to be turning ever more car-*dependent*. The different attempts in various parts of the country to encourage the citizenry to give up their cars and rely more on mass transit have not fared well, chiefly because of America's deeply ingrained love affair with the automobile. The flight of affluent Americans to the suburbs and rural areas makes that trend even less likely to take hold. There may be such things as luxury cars, but the car as a luxury per se is a long-dead notion. To keep pace with the many demands our society puts on the family unit, it is necessary that we remain mobile, and remain mobile on our own terms.

If we must buy cars, then we must. The purchase isn't cheap, however; in fact, it's getting more expensive all the time. When I was much younger, I remember people saying they would never pay more than $10,000 for a car. I have to wonder what those same people are driving now, because the cost of the average car (exclusive of interest, warranty, taxes, etc.) is just above $20,000; in 1965, the average cost was about $3500. This difference represents an average annual increase at a rate 1 1/2 times that of inflation. For most people the purchase of an automobile is second only to the purchase of a home in total cost, when you factor in both the principal amount and the interest on a typical car loan. Actually, it's not so uncommon anymore to find automobiles which cost considerably more than houses in lower-priced neighborhoods.

Most people who seek to buy a car enter the lion's den (the dealership) quite ill-prepared to minimize their losses. That's right, I didn't say "to bargain for a good deal"; I said "to minimize their losses," because in reality that's all you can do even when you try your best. That said, let's dig in.

FREEDOM PRINCIPLE
**Whenever possible, purchase your
car for cash.**

I realize that most people can't go out and pay for a new car without using a loan, but if you can, do it. This is the "dream" way to buy a car, in my opinion. Look at the $20,000 average automobile I referred to earlier. If you make a $3000 down payment and finance $17,000 of the purchase price over five years at 9% (a typical rate of interest), that $17,000 turns into well over $22,000, which means you will be paying over $5000 in interest!

Some people who can afford to pay cash still balk at putting so much of their money into an automobile at one time. I've actually heard some claim that because they can earn 12% to 15% on their mutual fund investments, it would make more sense to finance the car and pay out only 9%, therefore coming out 3% to 6% ahead. This faulty logic is cousin to a similar principle which is used by homebuyers. However, it makes sense when talking about a house. Why? What is the difference? The difference lies in the fact that cars *depreciate* in value, while houses *appreciate* in value.

Let's use an illustration to help demonstrate the difference. If you buy a $100,000 home with a mortgage loan at 9%, the chances are pretty fair that your home will be worth about $125,000 after five years. If you buy a $20,000 car with an auto loan at 9%, in five years you will probably still be making payments on a vehicle worth around $5000. It makes sense, then, to finance as little of the car price as you have to, no matter how great an interest rate you can secure on the loan.

In case financing a car doesn't appear unattractive enough, let me remind you of one other difference in our house-car comparison: Interest on a home loan is still deductible, as are the property taxes. Interest on auto loans is not deductible.

FREEDOM PRINCIPLE
**Don't buy a new car; instead buy one
which is two or three years old.**

This Principle is also related to the issue of depreciation. The startling fact is that a new car drops 30% to 40% in value once you drive it off the lot. This means that if you buy a $20,000 car it is worth only $12,000 to $14,000 before you even get it home. Depreciation is a terrible kick in the teeth for a new-car buyer; after only two years that $20,000 car will in some cases have declined between 50% and 70% in value. The loss in value will never again be as great as it is in the first two or three years of owning the car, however.

This is why I believe this Principle to be so sound. Let someone else suffer the 40% loss. Don't allow yourself to be taken in by the shiny new models which you may believe are calling your name. If you feel yourself being drawn to one of those, just remember the 40% kick in the teeth. Focus your car search on the cars you might have had your eye on two or three years ago.

FREEDOM PRINCIPLE
**Don't begin the car-buying process
until you know exactly what
you're looking for.**

If you ask someone who is is preparing to go car-shopping what he's looking for, you may get a response like "I don't really know for sure. I have my eye on several different models." Because most people can easily find themselves liking five or six different kinds of cars simultaneously, this answer may not be considered unusual. It can, however, create problems.

If you want to get the best deal you can (or rather, minimize your loss as much as possible), you must become focused and stay that way. If you start making your way into dealerships with several possibilities in mind, it will be easy for the salesman to sell you a bill of goods which you may not want for a price you *really* cannot afford. Why? Because you haven't made up your mind yet; you haven't dedicated your heart and mind to the purchase of one particular model of car. It will be easy for you to become confused during the process. I know there are lots of great cars out there, but you can't have them all. If you adapt the Principles you learn in this chapter to your search for one particular automobile, you should do well. Learning and living these Principles can help you minimize your losses on *any* car you look for; so save yourself the confusion and potential for vulnerability which can haunt anyone looking at more than one car at the same time. Do your homework, and then pick one!

CARS

FREEDOM PRINCIPLE
Determine the dealer cost of the vehicle you want before beginning the buying process.

This Principle could be "Part B" of the previous Principle. Once you have picked out exactly what you want, you will want to find out what the dealer paid for the car. Before you get on the showroom floor and find yourself locked into the negotiation process, you have to have some idea of the basis on which you're negotiating. My advice is to get a copy of any of the new-car pricing guides which are popular these days and to simply look up the car. The better guides will show you a side-by-side comparison of dealer invoice and retail price. Also, the guides should provide a breakdown of dealer invoice versus retail price on the available options as well. Your ultimate goal is to be able to purchase the car right at or even below dealer cost. It is sometimes possible to purchase a new car for a price just below dealer invoice. Why? Because, the factory will usually have built in a 2% to 5% commission in the invoice price for the dealer.

If you decide to follow the two-to-three-year-old car strategy, you won't be able to find the dealer's cost in a new-car guide. Instead, you will have to consult one of the many used-car guides which are in circulation these days. I would recommend that you refer to the *NADA Official Used Car Guide* at your local bookstore or library to obtain the most accurate price. This guide will provide you with several pieces of information, but there are two you should focus on in particular. One is the amount listed under "Average Trade-In," and the other is the amount listed under "Average Retail." The "Average Trade-In" price is similar to the dealer invoice price on a new car. The "Average Retail" price is similar to the retail price listed for a new car in a new car guide. The *NADA*

Official Used Car Guide, along with other pricing guides, can be found in the reference section of your local bookstore.

FREEDOM PRINCIPLE
Determine the accurate value
of your trade before starting the
shopping process.

Most people who shop for a new car will usually also be trying to sell their current vehicle. Whether they sell to the dealer as part of the new-car buying process or sell the car privately is up to them. However, in both cases, it's in your best interest to know precisely what your trade-in is worth, particularly when selling to the dealer.

An automobile dealer can make money on you in so many ways it's not funny. One easy way is to play off your trade against the purchase price of your new car. It works especially well on customers who attempt to play hardball on the price of the new car. Here's what happens: The salesman, seeing that you're someone who can't be fooled, allows you to see the dealer invoice you've been requesting on the new car you're considering. Sure enough, the price listed is exactly the same as the price you saw when you checked your new car guide. Now you want to be fair, so you allow the salesman to make a 3% commission on the price of the new vehicle. You throw in your trade, and the deal is done.

Wait a minute. What did you get for your trade? How do you know that the price you were given was fair? Too many people focus on the "front end" of the purchase transaction (the cost of the new vehicle) and pay no attention to the "back end" of the deal (the price received for the trade-in). Very often, "lowballing" you on your trade is how a salesman can make his money. Don't be tricked by focusing your attention exclusively on the shiny new car sitting in front of you; there's no law which states that only through that car may the sales-man make his commission. Consult your *NADA Official Used Car Guide* to know what is a fair price for your trade. Accept no less than the amount listed under "Average Trade-In." You might want to hold out for as much of the retail price listed as you can get. If you aren't satisfied with what you're being offered for your trade, hold on to it and sell it yourself. You'll almost always get a better deal anyway.

Actually, selling your trade yourself can be part of a smart car-shopping strategy. Tell the dealer from the outset that you may be trading in your current vehicle as part of the transaction. He will automatically begin to view the trade as a potential haven for profit. Play hardball on the price of the new vehicle, allowing the salesman to quote you a price for your trade which you *know* is below what it's worth. Get the salesman first to commit to a figure for the new car which does *not* include the trade. At this point you may decide that the price of the new car is indeed acceptable. This strategy will mean coming up with more up-front money in some cases, but if you can afford it, do it.

FREEDOM PRINCIPLE
**Always remember that haggling alone
represents no victory.**

Very often, people with little experience in car-buying feel they secured a good deal simply because they haggled over the price of the car. You should know that salesmen are well-trained to watch out for these sorts of people, and will gladly humor them while they play "hardball." The fact is that if you're haggling without any true facts in mind as to the dealer cost of what you're negotiating on, you're just wasting your time. By haggling with only the sticker price to focus on, you will feel you achieved victory when the salesman lets the car go for a few hundred dollars *below the sticker price.* You still probably paid about 18% over the invoice price, which means you paid about 15% too much. If you want to negotiate from a point of strength, at least know the dealer cost of what it is you're negotiating over.

FREEDOM PRINCIPLE
Beware of the "no-haggle" dealerships; you may still pay too much.

I happened to be looking through an auto-pricing guide one day and stumbled upon General Motors' Saturn. Saturn, as you may know, represents an experiment in "no-haggle" car buying. Many dealers are trying the Saturn approach around the country. The cars are priced fairly, according to Saturn, which eliminates the need for both parties in the transaction to haggle over the price. Saturn salesmen, in fact, are paid by salaries, not commissions. However, be advised that Saturn dealerships still mark up their vehicles by about 10–12% over invoice, which is 6–8% more than you should pay.

Is it really possible, then, to get a good deal at a fixed-price dealership? Probably not. Not only will you still pay more than you should for a new car, but the dealer can still try to make a big profit by shortchanging you on your trade-in. Again, consult the *NADA Official Used Car Guide* before you take your trade to *any* dealership. Don't allow any dealership to build an unreasonable amount of profit into the price they give you for the trade.

If you despise the negotiation process, then fixed-price dealers might be the place for you. After all, if you hate haggling that much, a typical, commission-based dealership is *certainly* not the place for you. Many Christians, for example, don't feel comfortable assuming the adversarial position which typical dealerships often place them in. If that is you,

CARS

and you honestly don't care about saving as much money as you can on the purchase of a car, then perhaps these "no-haggle" dealerships are right for you.

FREEDOM PRINCIPLE
Do not expect to "win" in the car
purchase process. All you can do is
incur less of a loss.

I often hear of people who come back from their car buying effort "knowing" that they received a "great deal." I maintain that it's not really possible to strike such a deal when you buy a car from a dealership. First, remember that we're talking about a highly depreciable asset. In fact, I don't know if "asset" is an appropriate word to attribute to a car. Because a car loses so much of its value in the first two to three years you own it, it seems impossible that you could ever truly get a "good deal," no matter how little you ended up paying.

The issue of depreciation aside, you still must wade through the sea of hidden charges, add-ons, stepped-up finance charges, trade-in rip-offs, and many other "profit centers" which make the whole experience so costly to the consumer. One of my financial counselors told me that a friend of his, back from an exhaustive round of car shopping, told him with disgust that it is *impossible* for anyone to get a good deal and that the only way you can win is if you bid the salesmen low enough that they let you walk out of the dealership. If you are able to strike a deal, no matter how much haggling is involved, then that means the dealership is the winner in most cases. But if you need a car, you're stuck with the fact that you must buy one. If you go to the trouble of trying to negotiate wisely, and simply view the whole process as a business transaction from which you want to derive the greatest benefit, then you will at least be able to hold your losses to a minimum. That should be your goal.

FREEDOM PRINCIPLE
Do not bypass the salesman in the buying process.

Some people, when car shopping, believe they will get a better deal if they circumvent the floor salesman altogether and deal directly with management. Their reasoning is that if the dealership doesn't have to pay out a commission, they will save money and pass that savings right along to the customer.

But it doesn't work that way. First, typical management doesn't want to be bothered dealing with a customer at the first level of the process. Once you've spent a few minutes chatting with a manager, he will still artfully turn you over to one of his "best men, who will truly take care of you, Mr. Jones." He will have smooth-talked you back into the clutches of the salesman, only now you may have bought into the manager's story and your guard is down.

The other reason it's not a good idea to go directly to management is that, by doing so, you have severely impaired your ability to negotiate. Let's say management *is* willing to deal with you. Does it not seem likely that, because you're confident you're dealing with the "bottom line" that there is a much greater chance you will accept whatever they tell you as the truth? Can't you hear it now? "Speaking as the sales manager, Mr. Jones, I can honestly tell you that this is as low as we can go." Even if you are "fortunate" enough to get in front of the dealership manager, you will undoubtedly get the same kind of story.

By going around the salesman, you have lost what can be a valuable tool in the bargaining process. The salesman, who is the liaison between you and management, can be dealt with more effectively in the negotiations; management will be less flexible. Do your homework on price, and then be content to deal with the first salesman who approaches you.

FREEDOM PRINCIPLE
**Never buy a car during your first
trip to the dealership.**

This one is a classic truth. If you buy a car during your first trip to the dealership, you probably got a bad deal. I know it's easy to find yourself tempted by all those shiny new cars in the lot and on the showroom floor, but fight the temptation. This is where you're going to need some discipline. There's so much distance that you will need to travel from the retail price to a fair price that in most cases you will not be able to travel all of it on your first visit.

FREEDOM PRINCIPLE
**If you want to save the most money, don't
buy your car through an auto broker.**

Automobile brokers bill themselves as tools you can use to save money on your car purchase. They will tell you that by purchasing your car through them, it's almost like purchasing directly from the factory. You won't have to involve yourself with the whole tiresome process of negotiating, and because a broker doesn't carry the overhead of a dealer you can get a great price on the vehicle. Doesn't sound like a bad idea, does it?

In truth, going through a broker probably won't save you much money, and the whole thing may be more trouble than it's worth. First, a broker doesn't work for free. There will be some type of brokerage fee, and that may be rather pricey.

Second, brokers have to arrange delivery of your vehicle through a local dealership. That dealership will also receive a fee for its trouble. Can you see what's happening? The middlemen you wanted to avoid by going with a broker are back in the equation; they just happen to be different middlemen.

There are other issues. A broker is exactly just that—a broker. His goal is to *sell* you a car, not take your used car into inventory. Most brokers do not have the means to dispose of used cars; usually it's new-car dealers that have either a used-car lot or an outlet through auto auctions.

Furthermore, if there's a problem with your car, you may have a tough time getting it resolved if you bought the car from a broker. The dealership that delivered your car through the broker did only that—deliver it. Most brokers do not honor repair warranties in the same way as auto dealerships. After buying a car from a broker you can try to go back and complain to the dealership if you have a problem, but they are not likely to be as accommodating as they would if the car had been purchased there directly.

FREEDOM PRINCIPLE
Don't buy the extended warranty or credit life insurance.

When you get to the dealership's finance department, you will get pitched on buying the extended warranty. The idea behind the extended warranty is that it picks up where the basic warranty coverage leaves off. For example, let's say the basic warranty on your new car will cover repairs for three years or 36,000 miles. The finance manager will tell you, "For just a few more dollars a month, you can increase the warranty coverage to five years or 60,000 miles." This type of extra coverage, at first glance, may seem reasonable enough. However, these extended policies rarely work out to your advantage.

CARS

First, you should know that the person who sells you the extended warranty makes a huge commission. I'm always suspicious of any insurance or insurance-type coverages which can afford to pay their salesmen enormous commissions. If the company can afford to pay out so much of what they take in for the coverage, what does that say about their expectations on how often you will use the coverage?

Second, most extended warranties are difficult to cash in. You may find yourself having to jump through hoops in order to meet the requirements for using it. I believe that most factory warranties are more than sufficient, without buying these add-ons. Instead of dealing with all of this, "self-insure" yourself for the maintenance expenses which exceed your factory warrant, which can come from a cash reserve fund. Set aside three to six months' worth of living expenses which can be used to meet any repair obligations or other emergency expenses which come up.

FREEDOM PRINCIPLE
**Don't arrange financing for your purchase
through the dealership.**

Here we go again. We love things quick and easy, and therefore we seem willing to pay a premium to have them that way. The financing of a car is no different. We can buy a car and arrange financing for it in the same place. What could be better than that?

A lot.

First, understand that you shouldn't finance a car with a dealer; you should finance it with a bank. The bank which deals through the particular dealership you're purchasing from will either provide a representative, an on-line computer service, or both to help facilitate the transaction. What you may not be aware of is that such loans represent additional profit opportunities to the dealerships, for the bank and the dealer have struck an agreement whereby the bank will finance all of the dealer's cars for a guaranteed minimum interest rate—say 9%. If the dealer can get you to pay an even higher rate, he keeps the difference. So if you have agreed to finance a car through the dealer at 11%, chances are that the bank is only seeing about 8% or 9%; the remainder goes to the dealer.

I would suggest that you always arrange financing *before* you begin shopping. Go to a local lender and get approved for a loan in the appropriate price range. The interest rate you pay will almost always be lower, and you will usually have about 60 days to make your choice. After that, assuming you were unable to make a decision in time, you will have to go back and renegotiate the loan. This is done to ensure that the bank is protected against a broad move in interest rates which might adversely affect their cost of money.

If you have the ability to use a credit union, I would certainly suggest going there first. Credit unions can typically offer more favorable rates because they are nonprofit, which means that they have no obligation to anyone other than their members. Banks, on the other hand, have shareholders who expect the bank to be earning a profit.

FREEDOM PRINCIPLE
Don't lease a car, it's not really
less expensive.

I'm tired of hearing about how leasing is such a great deal because it's less expensive than buying. That is a deception pushed on the American car-buying public through a slick media campaign. The only grain of truth to this is that your *monthly payments* will be lower if you lease, so now you can afford to *lease* a car you would not otherwise be able to *purchase*. The total cost to you, however, is going to be higher. If

CARS

you purchase a car with an open-end lease, you are on the hook for the residual, or remaining, value of the car which has yet to be paid for, *if* the dealer can't realize that value through the resale of the vehicle. This means that the current market value of the car may not be sufficient to pay off the amount still owed on the lease. If this is the case, you are then required to pay the "negative" balance.

Also, keep a close eye on the lease contract before you sign it. There are typically allowances for the dealer to charge you maintenance and excess mileage charges (which could be quite exorbitant). As important as it is to read the sales contract for an auto, it's even more important to read the leasing agreement. Dealers love to sneak in hidden charges. Don't sign a thing until you know precisely what it is you're getting. Leasing may make sense in some cases, especially if you're the sort of person who expects to make a car payment every month for the rest of his life. In this case a closed-end lease might be the way to go, because it allows you to simply turn in the car at the end of the lease period *without* being responsible for the residual value. You must, however, be forever content to throw your money down a guaranteed hole, without any hope of ever gaining any real value for your investment.

CARS

8

Should You Rent or Buy Your Home?

The truth about real estate transactions is sometimes difficult to get. Similar to auto purchases, most people are guilty to some degree of exaggerating the real truth about how good a deal they really finessed. This chapter will serve as a general overview of how to buy real estate for either investment purposes or as your personal residence.

BUYING VERSUS RENTING

As far as asset-building goes, in my financial planning practice I have found that most people have accumulated their wealth at retirement primarily from the equity in their home. Although it is true that real estate is no longer the "can't lose" investment it was once believed to be (evidenced by its crash in the eighties), it is still without question one of America's best investment opportunities. In terms of buying your own home versus renting, it is pretty clear that owning makes much more sense. First of all, you have to live somewhere so it is not a decision about spending or not spending money for a place to live, but only about how to spend the money. (This statement is not true if you, like many adults, live with your parents rent-free, which is a clearly superior strategy to buying or renting your own place!)

FREEDOM PRINCIPLE
In most economic cycles it is less
expensive to own real estate
than to rent it.

Buying real estate essentially involves two components: first, the property itself, which in most transactions involves both the land and a building, and second, the loan on the property. Most of the challenge involved in a real estate transaction is in the loan. The truth is that in most economic cycles it is less expensive to buy than to rent the same home over the long run. (One exception is when we're in the midst of an inflated real-estate market, where home prices escalate rapidly. In this case, you may be better off renting a house and putting money aside in savings until house prices drop.)

Another important benefit of home ownership is that you will experience an equity buildup that enhances your net worth. This is true because mortgage interest is fully tax-deductible, and so are real estate taxes. Most people, given the chance, would gladly buy a home and could typically afford the monthly payment. The problem, however, is usually related to the down payment and qualifying process of mortgage financing rather than the monthly payment, since after the tax benefits are factored in, owning is not much more expensive than renting, and in many cases it is actually less expensive. Let's review an example.

Assume that you are paying currently $800 per month in rent to live in a home that you can buy for approximately $80,000. To finance this property at 10% interest you would be paying $700 per month. Additionally, you would have the expenses of taxes and insurance. So your grand total monthly outflow of expenses would be about $900.

Remember, however, that your interest and real estate taxes are fully tax deductible on your federal tax return. So

HOME

this means approximately $10,000 in tax deductions for the year. This amount of tax deductions equals approximately $2800 in tax savings for people in the 28% tax bracket.

It is true that the amount you are allowed to deduct becomes less each year because your monthly payments focus less on paying off interest and more on paying off the principal. However, you will still continue to see a real savings in your personal finances because your monthly payments stay the same during the life of the loan, whereas if you rented a house you can be sure your monthly payments will increase almost yearly. Even using a conservative increase annually in the cost of renting (let's say 4%), the rental cost of $800 per month could increase to almost $1100 per month by year five of our hypothetical comparison. The real clincher is to know that with home ownership, someday you will have no mortgage payment at all to make. Furthermore, the fact that your property has increased in value dramatically and you own it debt-free is even more icing on the cake.

FREEDOM PRINCIPLE
**Rent if you are planning to live in an area
for less than three years.**

As you can see, owning (versus renting) is most likely the way to go for you. There are some exceptions, however. For example, if you are planning to live in an area for only a short time (less than three to four years), owning is probably not a good idea, since the transaction costs of buying and selling will most likely cancel out any real profits on price appreciation and then some. Also, if you are new to an area you will most likely become a more informed buyer and consequently get a better deal if you rent for six months, or until you are familiar with the area and the real estate prices. I do not see how a person can fly into a city and buy a home after only two or three

HOME

weekends of looking and expect to get a good deal. I'm not saying it can't be done, but only that it is highly unlikely.

THE DOWN PAYMENT PROBLEM

As mentioned earlier, the idea of home ownership is attractive to just about everyone. So why do we not all own our homes? There are probably a number or reasons, but the most likely is what I call the "down payment problem." Some of the others include poor credit, inconsistent work history, lack of commitment to one's financial future, and fear of the process.

FREEDOM PRINCIPLE
Don't limit yourself to the idea that saving
enough for a down payment is the only
way you will ever get a home.

One of the best-selling business books in history is one written in 1980 and titled *No Money Down,* by Robert Allen. This book began a wave of no-money-down teaching on the subject of creative financing strategies for real estate buyers. In fact, even today some of the same teachers are going strong with their books and tapes and seminars. It is clear, however, that the high level of interest that was present in the early eighties is now gone. I am asked many times about no-money-down approaches on my radio show, and with great surprise to my listeners I explain that these ideas are valid and can still be implemented today. The concept of buying real estate with no money down is relatively easy to grasp, since in essence all we are doing is finding a way to buy a home or investment property without any cash out of our pocket. The following are the three most common approaches.

1. **Assumable financing combined with an owner-financed second mortgage.** FHA and VA mortgages issued in

1986 and earlier are fully assumable without qualifying. What this means is that the only requirement is being above the age of majority (often 18) in your state. There is no income verification or even the requirement that you are employed. Furthermore, you can even have had bad credit or no credit at all, because your credit report is never even checked, since the loan has no qualifying requirements whatsoever. I purchased my second home in this way.

The challenge that most people face in these kinds of transactions is what I call the equity problem. Since these mortgages can only be assumable without qualifying if they were issued in 1986 or prior, this often creates a problem, because the property may have appreciated in value substantially. As the property goes up in value the mortgage balance declines because the current owner continues to make his monthly payment. The original purchase may have been for $100,000 and the property may now be worth $110,000. The monthly payments (plus the original down payment) have reduced the balance owed to only $90,000 after four or five years. While it is true that one can assume such a mortgage without qualifying, even after assuming the mortgage there is still a $20,000 equity that the owner will want to be paid for.

In these cases, if you have a truly motivated seller you can begin the process of negotiating for a second mortgage between you and the owner. The ways such a second mortgage can be structured are really unlimited. As an example, I purchased a home like this in 1986 and got the owner to carry the second mortgage for three years while I simply made an extra payment each month to him until the second mortgage was paid off. In some cases I have had clients make monthly payments against both the first and second mortgages for a period of one to two years and then get conventional financing through a bank. (That is, they refinance their loan and combine both mortgages into just one.) This is easy to accomplish, since in a year or two the appreciation of the property as well as the

HOME

reduction of the mortgage balance can create enough of a margin for a bank to be interested in providing conventional financing.

I could easily write an entire chapter on conventional bank financing, but the bottom line is that the more equity you have in a property the easier it is to qualify for a loan. In some scenarios where a buyer puts down 30% or more there may be very minimal income and employment requirements, if any.

FREEDOM PRINCIPLE
Owner financing can be an excellent
investment for the seller and a great
source of financing for the buyer.

2. Owner financing. This method of buying a home without a down payment means that the owner agrees to let you pay him directly in monthly installments, thus circumventing the need for a bank loan. This is a possibility when the owner of a property has no mortgage balance. This strategy has been hard to accept by many of my seminar attendees. After all, why would someone finance a property that he owns debt-free? Would he not need the money to buy his next property?

A very typical example is an an older couple who are planning to retire and sell the large home that they raised their children in to move to a smaller home or condominium in a retirement community. In many scenarios, one of their greatest areas of concern is how to take the assets they have accumulated during their lifetime and put them into an investment plan that creates a steady income for their retirement years. This is the key to arranging one of these deals. If you can show a retired couple a good enough reason to finance the property, they may go ahead and do it. If they become the "bank" in the transaction they can have an attorney structure a mortgage agreement and begin receiving monthly income at an interest rate well above what CDs and bonds would pay them.

Remember, the secret to negotiation is understanding the needs of the other person. In this situation the need is *income* rather than a lump sum. If you can show the sellers how to get what they want and still arrange the transaction to get what *you* want, it becomes a win-win arrangement for both parties. Although it is very common to find this arrangement with retired people, you may also find investors at any age who understand the benefit of self-financing these deals. But if you don't ask you won't get, so at least explore the possibilities of this kind of financing.

FREEDOM PRINCIPLE
Lease purchase agreements provide
you with the benefits of owning and the
flexibility of renting.

HOME

3. **Lease purchase agreements.** To some degree this is a last resort, to be used if either the no-down method or owner financing cannot be agreed upon. However, this type of transaction still provides many benefits to the buyer and the seller. The agreement is very simple: The prospective buyer agrees to lease the property for a specified period of time, usually one to five years. During this lease period he has the right to buy the home at any time based on an agreed-on-in-advance option price. The second element to the agreement is to negotiate a portion of the monthly lease payment to the owner to be recognized as a credit at closing toward the purchase of the home. For example, if you are paying $1000 a month in rent you might negotiate that $200 of the $1000 be applied toward the eventual purchase of the property. After five years (60 months × $200) you would have a buildup of $12,000 for your down payment.

Another interesting consideration is that the agreed-on option price is usually based on the *current* value of the property at the time the lease option agreement is signed. What this means is that in addition to the buildup of a down payment you will also have an intrinsic equity because of likely appreciation of the value of the property from the date you purchased it. A likely scenario might be a home with a value of $100,000 appreciating to be worth perhaps $120,000 over a five-year period. Add this amount to the $12,000 from the rent credit and you now have $32,000 "equity" as your down payment in terms of how the bank will look at the deal. This gives you more than a 25% down payment, making it a very easy-to-finance deal.

This type of approach is very attractive to sellers who are desperate to get rid of a property that is sitting vacant for any number of reasons. Probably the most common situation when this makes sense is in the case of a job transfer, where an individual is relocated to another city and is now forced into making two payments, one on his new home and the other on the home that has yet to be sold. If he has purchased a new home already, you can conclude that he doesn't need the proceeds from his other home for that purpose, and thus you can deliver him two benefits he wants and needs—the relief from making two home payments plus a likely future buyer for his property.

Remember that a lease option is an *option*. You do not have to exercise your option to buy, which is another great benefit that allows you the flexibility to change your mind if it turns out that you do not want to buy the house. This approach gives you many of the benefits of owning, but with the opportunity to change your mind. Many real estate experts advise this approach as a way to "test drive" a property before you make the decision to buy. The idea of leasing with an option to buy for even a short period of time (perhaps one year) gives you the opportunity to get a feel for the neighborhood and the house. I recently moved to Dallas and negotiated a lease-purchase option on a house that I thought I might want to buy. But after a year we determined that the house is too old and needs handyman work too frequently. My option to buy will not be exercised, and we will move to another home in North Dallas instead.

INCREASING YOUR CHANCES OF SUCCESS

FREEDOM PRINCIPLE
Consider 50 to 100 properties
before buying one.

The only way to get a bargain when shopping for real estate is to look at a large number of properties, and I mean large. Most of the writers on the subject will tell you to look at 50 to 100 properties before making your decision. It is hard not to get a good deal after looking at this number of properties. Don't get discouraged after trying to find a creatively financed deal after looking at only a handful of properties.

FREEDOM PRINCIPLE
Call 100 property owners to find
20 prospects for a creative financing
transaction. Out of these 20 prospects
will come two or three deals.

Remember, the key to finding creatively financed real estate is in the numbers. In most cases you will not find properties with creative financing options if you look only at small quantities of property for sale. It is not uncommon for seasoned real estate investors to look at hundreds of properties

HOME

over a six-to-eight-month period before finding that "special deal" they will buy.

FREEDOM PRINCIPLE
**Make qualifying phone calls before you
visit any property personally.**

To save time, be sure to contact the owner prior to visiting the property to determine if there is really a deal there or not. Some questions you should ask the seller include:

1. Could you please tell me about your home? (Size, square footage, lot size, garage, how many bedrooms, bathrooms, etc.)
2. What type of existing financing is in place? Do you have an assumable mortgage? What is the interest rate and the monthly payment?
3. Would you be able to help with the financing?
4. Will you need cash at closing or would it be possible to spread the down payment over a period of time?
5. Would you consider making the property available with a lease option arrangement?
6. What is the asking price for your home and how long has it been on the market?

Remember that this is a numbers game. Don't be surprised if almost everyone you talk to says no to assisting on the financing or working with you on a down payment. Keep in mind that you are not trying to buy every property on the market. There are only a select few that you can buy and make money on.

FREEDOM PRINCIPLE
**Protect yourself from costly surprises
by completing the property disclosure
sheet (shown below) when you visit
the property (listed below).**

PROPERTY DISCLOSURE SHEET

Property Address: _____

_____

	Yes	No	Unknown
1. What is the approximate age of the roof? _____ *years*	___	___	___
2. To your knowledge, has the roof ever leaked?	___	___	___
3. Has the roof ever been repaired by you or anyone else?	___	___	___
4. Is there a guarantee in effect on your roof?	___	___	___
5. Does the property have any filled ground?	___	___	___
6. Do you know of any past or present land settling problems on your property?	___	___	___
7. Has the property ever had a drainage or flooding problem?	___	___	___
8. Is the property in a designated flood zone?	___	___	___
9. Do you have or know of any inspections, reports or surveys concerning this property?	___	___	___
10. Does anyone have a right of refusal or option lease on the property?	___	___	___
11. Do you know of any existing or pending legal action concerning this property?	___	___	___

HOME

	Yes	No	Unknown

12. Do you know of any condition in the original or existing design or workmanship of the structure that would be considered substandard?   ____   ____   ____

13. Are you aware of any heating, electrical, or mechanical systems in your property that are in need of repair or replacement?   ____   ____   ____

14. Do you know of any violations of government regulations or ordinances with regard to this house?   ____   ____   ____

HOME

FREEDOM PRINCIPLE
Visit the county courthouse to determine
what properties are selling for in
a neighborhood.

In order to determine fair market value, there is truly no better method than the "comparable method." Real estate appraisers use as their primary basis for valuing property the sales of similar homes that have taken place in that same neighborhood. Real estate sales are a matter of public record, and you will find this information easy to get from the public records office, where you will find a clerk who can help you access the information you need. An additional resource that I would recommend is "The Carlton Sheets Real Estate Home Study Course." This course costs approximately $200, and you can find out more information about it by writing to the Professional Education Institute, 8160 S. Madison, Burr Ridge, IL 60521.

It is very important to be persistent, and even more important to be creative when looking for a home. The deals are out there, but you have to be persistent and creative to make them work. Because of the popularity of this topic, I have developed a series of easy-to-use workbooks that provide supplemental training on creative real-estate transactions. You can find out more about these workbooks by calling 1-800-877-2022.

HOME

9

WHEN COLLEGE IS COMING

While I was in college, money was a sparse commodity for me, to say the least. As an on-campus resident I would get three meals a day, Monday through Friday, but no meals were provided on the weekend. This created an interesting dilemma each Friday night, which would be my last meal until Monday morning's school-provided breakfast. Even in those early days I had developed a few financial strategies, more from a survival instinct than from ingenuity.

On Saturdays at lunchtime, five or six of my friends and I would go to a local "all-you-can-eat" buffet, which at that time cost about $3.50. Our one-meal-a-day strategy was pretty basic: On Saturday we would simply wait to eat until lunchtime and then eat enough to last until Sunday, and repeat the strategy. This approach provided us with meals on the weekends for only about $7.00, which still left us with $2.00 to $3.00 for the weekend to buy gas or whatever.

As a college student I worked at a variety of different jobs and used student loans, grants, scholarships, and any other possible source to squeak my way through from semester to semester. My parents were not able to help me pay for my college education because of the financial challenges that they were facing at the time. Consequently, it has been my desire to provide my children with a fully paid college education. But in order to do that I realized I had to start early. All of our children from the day they were born have had an investment account that is building for their future college expenses. Although I would never want to go through the tough experience of my college days again, I know that those were the years when God had the opportunity to build character in me and to teach me to rely on Him.

Seeing children graduate from college is the dream of many parents throughout the United States (and around the world as well). And there's a good reason for that dream, for in the United States a college degree typically represents about a million dollars of additional income over the course of a lifetime compared to the income of a person who has no more than a high school diploma. Furthermore, the satisfaction which results from successfully completing a journey into the world of higher education can be a strong magnet as well. Many people pursue the college option to prepare for the life challenges which lie ahead.

Actually, these challenges can come at any age. More and more people are realizing that going to college is not simply a pursuit reserved for the young. College classrooms can now be found which contain everyone from fresh-faced teenagers right out of high school to senior citizens who want to take advantage of the opportunity they had to wait 40 or 50 years for.

There has been a fair amount of discussion in recent years about the usefulness of a college education in today's job market. While this chapter is not an essay on the pros and cons of going to college, I will address that issue briefly, since it comes up from time to time on my radio show. Simply put, I believe that pursuing a college degree is still a most appropriate expenditure of one's time and money. If you or your child aspires to gain access to the world's most respected vocations, a college degree is really a must. Take a doctor, for example. Do you know of any doctors who have never earned a college degree? How about lawyers? Can you be a lawyer today without possessing a degree? Can you become an engineer or an accountant without having earned a degree in those respective disciplines? With a few unusual exceptions, the answer to each of these questions is a resounding "No!" If you aspire to work as a professional, you must have a professional education.

In fact, a trend I've noticed developing in the last several years involves professions requiring degreed participants where no such requirement existed before. If you want to be a school gym teacher, for example, many school systems now require that you have a degree in Physical Education. Librarians now must have degrees in Library Science. If you want to work as a restaurant manager for a large company, you'd better have a degree in either Business or Food Services. One of my employees, fresh out of college, decided he wanted to become a police officer. He believed his college degree would give him a leg up on the competition. As he proceeded through the application process, however, he realized that several other applicants also had college degrees and that the department usually limited its final selections to the candidates who had them. My point should be clear by now: If you want to reap much of the financial bounty and security which the world's professions have to offer, go to college (or see that your child does).

Now I must throw in somewhat of a disclaimer. If you go to college with little notion of what you would like to do with the rest of your life, and end up earning a degree in a discipline which is not very marketable in the real world, you probably *will* feel that your education was little more than a waste of time and money. The responsibility for that, however, rests squarely on your shoulders. You may find that it is in your best interest to study something you're not wild about and work in a profession which is lucrative but may not be as personally pleasing as you would like.

COLLEGE

The earning of that career opportunity comes with two price tags, though. One price tag can be satisfied only with diligence and hard work. The other price tag can be only satisfied with money—lots of it. A four-year degree at a typical state university costs about $30,000 to $40,000, when all associated costs are considered. For a private university, the numbers can be downright frightening. If you can get out of four years at a private college for under $50,000, you're lucky. For some of the best, the cost can be as high as $100,000.

As if these figures aren't daunting enough, I have more news for you which you're not going to like: The costs are continuing to rise. In fact, the cost of college is increasing at the rate of 8% per year, roughly twice that of inflation. Why that situation exists is a mystery to some extent. I have heard a good theory, and it's based on the notion that colleges, unlike factories, don't lend themselves nearly as well to the contraction phase of economic cycles. That is, the college equivalent of laying off workers and requiring those that remain to work large amounts of overtime is not feasible, for a whole host of reasons.

Be that as it may, if you want to go to college it will cost you plenty. For the purposes of our discussion here, I'm not going to spend a lot of time talking about loans. The reason for this is that both high schools and colleges have ample resources to assist you on the subject of going into debt. What I *will* say on this subject is that your first step, before you do anything else, should be to contact the Federal Student Aid Information Center and request a copy of the *Student Guide to Financial Aid*. The guide is free and can be requested by writing to:

Federal Student Aid Information Center
P.O. Box 84
Washington, DC 20044

For purposes of discussion in this chapter, I will be talking as though I'm speaking to parents of college-bound children. If this offends you in some way, I can only apologize in advance, because these same strategies work for parents as well.

FREEDOM PRINCIPLE
**For best results, estimate the cost of your
child's education as early as possible.**

One of the long-standing rules of smart planning is to do it as early as possible. It doesn't really matter what's being planned—your retirement, a vacation, even a dinner party. The financing of a college education is really no different. The first order of business, when it comes to this topic, is for you to get an idea of how much money you will need at the appointed time. To get a general idea, you can simply work with the following values: $35,000 and $80,000. The cost of a four-year state university education is roughly $35,000. These days, $80,000 is a typical sum for a private university. Remember, though, that the cost of college is going up about 8% per year. You will want to decide which type of university you're going to shoot for, and determine how much you'll need to cover whatever the cost is at that time. To do this properly, I suggest that you use a financial calculator. I discuss how to use the financial calculator in Chapter 11, so you may want to refer to that section briefly right now.

Let's say you've decided that you want to send your child to a private university someday, and your child is currently two years old. Assuming the child goes to college at age 18, you have 16 years to save and invest. If one year of a private university education is about $20,000 ($80,000 divided by 4), the first order of business is to determine what that $20,000

COLLEGE

figure will be in 16 years, accounting for college-cost inflation. Key in the following values on your financial calculator:

PV (Present Value):	$20,000
% I (Annual Inflation Rate):	8
N (Number of Years):	16

The resulting calculation ("Compute" FV [future value]) tells you that the $20,000 of today will be $68,518 in 16 years. Multiply that figure by four years of college and you'll quickly see that a four-year private university education in 16 years will cost about $275,000. (That isn't precisely correct, as we haven't accounted for the inflationary effect on the sophomore-, junior-, and senior-year costs, but let's not worry about that here.) That $275,000 figure may be startling, but at least you know what you're up against so that you may plan accordingly. Actually, a more precise way to figure the cost is to select several schools which you believe may be good future possibilities, find out what each one costs today, and do the computation over again. I apologize if you're getting a bit bogged down in numbers right now, but it is important that you understand that this task must be approached with forethought if you're going to be successful in completing it.

Step 2 of this preliminary planning is to consider more closely the goal figure you've arrived at. Will you personally try to pay for all of it, some of it, or none of it? This is an essential part of the planning, because it is here that you actually settle on a goal figure to try to reach through your own efforts. Let's say your goal figure is $100,000. Using the number of years from the last example (16) and assuming an investment rate of return of 12% per year, how much money would you have to set aside each month to reach the goal? Here we go again with the financial calculator:

PV (present value): 0 (We'll assume you've set aside nothing so far.)

FV (future value): $100,000

% I (interest): 1 (12% ÷ 12 months)

N: 192 (16 years × 12 months. Remember, you're trying to determine a *monthly* figure.)

By computing the payments, you can see that you'll have to put away $173.73 per month to reach the $100,000 mark in the desired time.

I know I've thrown a lot at you here, but I want you to see how absolutely important it is to get a handle on what you're doing as soon as possible. The longer you wait to begin setting money aside, the more likely it is that you won't make it.

FREEDOM PRINCIPLE
**Steer clear of Savings Bonds, CDs, and
other traditional low-return choices when
making your college investment plans.**

I'm still amazed that after all these years many people (including some investment professionals) believe that Savings Bonds (Series EE bonds) are the ideal choice for college investing. The highest rate of return guaranteed by the bonds is currently about 5% per year. What did I tell you the inflation rate for college expenses was? 8%. I guess you can see the problem. Not only are you not beating the inflation rate, but you're finishing well behind it, which means you're really losing money. The same problem exists with CDs, even those "college" CDs pushed by some lending institutions. The rates of return just aren't sufficient. Sure, some of these investments may offer slightly higher returns than other similar types of vehicles, but so what? Determining that your 5% return is better than some other person's 4% is a hollow victory at best. Unless you are invested in the types of vehicles which can keep pace (at least) with the college expense inflation rate, you're in the wrong place.

There is one exception to what I've just said, and it exists out of deference to the time factor. If you begin putting money away only three or four years before it's needed, you might have to stick with one of the above-mentioned investments. The reason is that the types of investments which can earn double-digit returns are based in the stock market, and putting money in the market should only be done by long-term investors (about five years and longer) so that the temporary downswings can be accounted for without difficulty. You can see why it's important to start planning for your child's college costs *now*. The more time you have to keep the money invested, the better your investment options will be (and, ultimately, the greater the return on your money).

FREEDOM PRINCIPLE
Use stock mutual funds as your best
choice for long-term college investing.

What kind of investments can realize an average rate of return of at least 8% when evaluated over a period of several years? Stock market-based investments. There really isn't any other type of legitimate vehicle available which can so reliably achieve that kind of result. The average return of the market as a whole over the past 80 years—through both good and bad market cycles—has been about 11% per year. While it's possible that stocks are not the most attractive investment option at the time of this reading, be aware that market down-swings generally do not last more than a year or two. Over the long haul you'll always come out ahead.

What is the safest, smartest way to invest in the market? With no-load mutual funds. It's safe because each fund is made up of 50 to 100 different stocks (so risk is minimized) and smart because you're: a) not paying a commission and b) allowing your investment to be guided by a professional money manager who has the time and training to make well-informed investment choices on your behalf. A high-quality, no-load stock mutual fund should be able to average a return of about 12% per year. More aggressive stock funds have been known to do well over 20% in some years. I don't want to ignore the fact that mutual funds will fluctuate in performance from year to year, but investing for several years will ensure that your results are as competitive as possible.

FREEDOM PRINCIPLE
**Watch out for the special college
investment plans offered by some
mutual fund companies.**

Some mutual fund companies are beginning to get involved in marketing particular funds or developing certain programs which are designed "especially for the college investor." While I am obviously a big fan of mutual funds, make certain that the actual funds which are used in the given plan(s) are appropriate. Sometimes the fund family will only allow you to use its most conservative stock funds in this kind of program. If that's okay with you, great. However, the longer you're investing, the more aggressive you'll probably want to go. Bottom line: Even where mutual funds are con-cerned, don't get taken in by special college investment

COLLEGE

gimmicks. Select the funds which you know to be best for your investment objectives.

FREEDOM PRINCIPLE
If you will be age 59½ or older when your child goes to college, consider a variable annuity for college investing.

A variable annuity is a tax-deferred investment which is available from a life insurance company. Tax-deferred simply means that your investment earnings are allowed to build up in your account without being taxed until they are withdrawn. This tax-free compounding effect is called *tax deferral*. (Remember that you will pay taxes ultimately when you take the money out to enjoy it.) Within the annuity you may select from a number of mutual-fund-type options. Because annuities are designed to be tax-deferred retirement programs, you will be penalized by the IRS on any monies withdrawn before age 59½, just as with your Individual Retirement Account.

Although I know of many financial counselors who feel an annuity is a poor choice for college investing, that opinion is based on the assumption that you as an investor will withdraw the money before you're 59½ and get stuck with the penalty. That *would* be a bad idea. I'm always a fan of getting tax-deferred growth when you can, but to do so and then be hit with the IRS penalty of 10% is a waste in most cases. Because of the age considerations, annuities may be more appropriate for grandparents who wish to help with the savings process.

Here's one last thing I want to mention. Because variable annuities are available through life insurance companies, their investment options may not always be the greatest. Very often the mutual funds presented are no more exciting than the insurance company's own offerings. Before you sign up with a variable annuity, be sure that the fund choices are representative of at least some of the no-load families listed in Appendix C.

FREEDOM PRINCIPLE
Don't set up a Uniform Gifts to Minors
Act (UGMA) account if you want
to maintain a complete say in how
the money is spent in your
child's education fund.

One of the most popular types of investment accounts for college investing is the Uniform Gifts to Minors Act account or UGMA account. The UGMA account is like the Individual Retirement Account (IRA) in that it is not a particular type of investment in and of itself; it is the "umbrella" under which a wide variety of investments may be placed. Also like the IRA, the UGMA offers a favorable tax situation to investors, although it's not nearly as exciting. In a UGMA, the first $600 of earnings is taxed at the child's rate (15%). Earnings above $1200 are taxed at the parent's rate until the child reaches age 14, at which time the earnings are again taxed at the child's rate.

If you haven't figured it out thus far, the UGMA account is titled in the name of the child. You, the parent, serve as the custodian of the account. You are responsible for acting prudently in your role as custodian; you make all the decisions as to how the money in the account is to be invested. Once the child reaches the age of 18, control of the account reverts to him alone.

Setting up UGMA accounts is a pretty popular thing to do, and there are even investors who set up brokerage and mutual fund accounts in their children's names as a matter of course, just to get the tax breaks. Personally, I'm not as excited about UGMA accounts as other people are. I have a real

COLLEGE

problem with the fact that once the child reaches age 18, the full control of the account becomes his. Even I, Jim Paris, can remember a time when I wasn't so careful with a dollar and that time was right around the age of 18. I shudder to think what I might have done if I had been given my own highly valued mutual fund account.

The other problem with UGMA accounts pertains to financial aid. Typically, the financial aid offices of colleges and universities will require that about 40% of such investments titled in a child's name be designated as spendable on college expenses. Conversely, less than 10% of the parents' assets are required to be spent on the college expenses. These percentages are used to determine how much aid a prospective student may qualify for. So if you're counting on relying heavily on financial aid for your child, remember: The less you are perceived as having to spend on college, the more aid you will potentially receive. In this situation, you will probably want to forgo the UGMA account altogether.

FREEDOM PRINCIPLE
Don't view prepaid tuition plans as the automatic answer to your college funding investment woes.

More and more states are developing programs which allow their residents to prepay the tuition costs for attending their respective colleges and universities. Typically, the plans allow you to pay with either a lump-sum contribution or on a schedule of monthly payments, similar to any other type of traditional investment vehicle. You may initiate the plan at any time; however, it should come as no surprise to you that the earlier you begin, the better off you'll be. Once you've held up your end of the bargain, your child will be assured of receiving the four years of college you have diligently planned for *without* having to incur any other tuition costs. The costs associated with room and board are usually borne by you, although some states are now developing plans which permit you to account for those expenses as well.

My feelings with regard to these kinds of plans are mixed. I believe they have some merit *if* you are certain that your child will be attending a state school and *if* you would otherwise consider only low-paying vehicles (EE bonds, CDs, money markets, etc.) for your independent savings purposes. However, these kinds of plans have minuses which you must consider. First, if you don't stick to the program and your child attends school elsewhere, you'll have to face refund policies which can be quite unfavorable. Most states won't return much more to you than your principal, which certainly represents a poor return on your investment.

Speaking of investment return, that brings up another issue. I still haven't seen anything I like as well as stock mutual funds for long-term investing. By selecting your own high-quality portfolio of growth and aggressive growth funds, you can realize a return on your money that really can't be matched through any other means. Furthermore, the mutual fund investments you make on your own can be used anywhere, for any school. You retain full control of your principal as well as the interest it earns.

There's one more issue to consider, and I believe it's quite significant. As prepaid tuition plans began to gain in popularity, the IRS found a way to get a piece of the action. Even though you would be funding this program with after-tax dollars, the IRS has determined that you must be taxed again on the "growth" of your investment. That is, they contend that the difference between your principal investment and what the tuition costs when your child finally enters school can fairly be considered growth, which must now be taxed.

I believe that, all things considered, there are better ways to prepare for your child's college education than committing to the restrictive prepaid tuition plans. Although they may be satisfactory under certain circumstances, I would investigate the suitability of all other options before signing up.

FREEDOM PRINCIPLE
Go to the trouble of investigating private
scholarships and grant sources.

Clearly, the most underused resource in college financing is the scholarship. If you think it's underused because few qualify, you're wrong. It's underused because few *apply*. There is a great deal of confusion out there regarding where to look, who qualifies, and what it takes to apply. The fact is that well over 50% of the money which is available for financial aid to students comes from sources *other* than federal, state, or local governments. One of the most surprising statistics I've ever seen has to do with the small amount of private scholarship money used relative to the total amount available. At my last check it was less than 10%.

There are three reasons for this. First, most people who know these options exist have no clue where to find them. For the longest time it was impossible to tap into a bank of information which would allow a grant seeker to get a clear view of what was available. No one had bothered to go through the painstaking process of assembling a comprehensive list of these resources. Some sources are doing that now, and I'll speak about that in a minute.

Second, many people appear to have preconceived notions about who may qualify for this money. Some believe you must be poor and a member of a minority group; others believe that this money will only go to students who carried a 4.0 grade point average throughout high school. These notions are quite incorrect. Most private monies don't have as requirements either a strong academic record or dire economic need.

Finally, most people don't have a clue about how to apply. I've always found it odd that many private corporations and organizations who go to the trouble of assembling these programs in the first place leave you in the dark about how to access them. Most people who *do* try to pursue these grants and scholarships find themselves running into dead ends when they call the sponsoring organizations for more information.

What can *you* do to get your hands on the money that's out there? How can you locate the sources and find out exactly what it takes to apply? Personally, I believe that one of the best methods available is to access one of the many books and manuals which have been published for the express purpose of passing out this information. Several authors and editors, recognizing the need for this information, have gone to the trouble of compiling it and presenting it in a very thoughtful, user-friendly fashion. It is simply up to you to get these directories and sift through all the options, extracting the opportunities which apply to you or your particular situation.

If you would like to take your quest one step further, I encourage you to use one of the better scholarship search services which are available. For a fee, these services will assemble a biographical profile on the child and his family, and then feed that profile into a computer bank which has stored in it an enormous amount of information on private money resources. The printout which is generated contains the sources for which your child qualifies, based on the biographical data. Perhaps the most professional and comprehensive of these services is the National Scholarship Research Service (NSRS). The president of NSRS, Daniel J. Cassidy, has been a frequent guest on my radio show. To find out more about the services offered by NSRS, call 707-546-6777.

COLLEGE

FREEDOM PRINCIPLE
Consider the military option as an answer
to your college financing problems.

Here's something you may not be aware of: Did you know that the college funding programs available through the military represent the greatest source of money earmarked for that purpose (exclusive of need-based programs)? It's true, and that money can be accessed in a number of different ways.

First, the military reinstituted a scaled-down version of the old GI Bill several years ago. The original GI Bill, designed to assist returning World War II veterans, basically paid the full ride, regardless of where the student ended up going to school. The best version of this Bill available today is in the U.S. Army, where a four-year enlistment can provide a return of well over $30,000 in college money. Sizable amounts are also available for shorter enlistments, as well as for service in the Army Reserve. This option, used in conjunction with long-term investment planning, can give you the opportunity to fully pay for a college education without having to go one dime into debt.

A member of my staff used this method to get through a private university he otherwise would not have been able to afford without going deeply into debt. In addition to his college education, he also had an opportunity to travel throughout the world and enjoy a number of experiences he simply would have been unable to try anywhere else. Furthermore, he tells me that his record of military service has always been well-received by employers.

Another way your child can get money for college from the military is by enrolling in ROTC (Reserve Officers Training Corps). ROTC programs are sponsored by each of the major branches of the armed services and are available on a great number of college campuses throughout the United States. As a college student enrolled in ROTC, your child would be required to participate in special classes which teach leadership, military history, and other subjects considered essential to the training of a military officer. The summers between school years are typically spent attending various types of field training, and upon graduation your child would be commissioned as an officer in his respective branch of participation.

As far as the money goes, there can be plenty. Students can earn full, four-year ROTC scholarships, and there are also three- and two-year scholarships available. There are also financial benefits available to students who are *not* recipients of formal scholarships but are still enrolled in ROTC. The office of college planning/counseling in your child's high school will have more information on these programs, or you may write to the following addresses to request further assistance:

Navy/Marine Corps ROTC
250 Dallas Street
Naval Air Station
Pensacola, FL 32508-5220

College Army ROTC
Gold QUEST Center
Department PG92
P.O. Box 3279
Warminster, PA 18974-9872

Air Force ROTC
HQ/RROO
551 East Maxwell Boulevard
Maxwell Air Force Base, AL 36122-6106

Probably the most financially favorable way to access the military's money for college is also the most demanding. Young men and women who attend one of the nation's Service Academies will receive a guaranteed full ride through school and will also receive a monthly salary. A degree from one of these institutions is highly revered, but be forewarned: Your child will attend school for four years in a strict, military environment and will incur a lengthy service obligation upon graduation. Furthermore, the competition for available slots is fierce, to say the least. Candidates must be appointed by a Congressman in order to gain entrance.

COLLEGE

Higher education is indeed expensive, but there are ways to meet the cost without taking a trip to the poorhouse. I hope I've been able to shed a little light on some of the methods you and your family can use to make this dream a reality. The key is to *focus on the goal early* and to *remain committed*.

COLLEGE

10

THE FINANCIAL
SIDE OF DIVORCE

Being a radio talk show host is a unique experience, to say the least. Every day at 3:00, I get to speak to hundreds of thousands of people across America through the magic of radio. What's more, they get to talk back to me, which makes things very interesting at times. Over the years, having answered thousands of questions from radio listeners around America, I have developed the ability to anticipate questions even before they are totally asked by a caller. Usually within the first four or five words of a caller's opening statement, I can predict exactly what his or her question will be. Over the past two or three years I have found that the word "divorce" is closely followed by such phrases as "my credit is ruined, I have filed for personal backruptcy, my home is in foreclosure, I'm losing my business, I owe money to the IRS."

Something seems to happen, in terms of money, within a family that experiences a divorce. I have never been divorced and don't plan to ever have that experience. And this chapter is certainly not an endorsement of divorce. Being a realist, however, and understanding that statistically in America today, one of every two new marriages will end in divorce, I feel compelled to share with you how to go through a divorce without also going broke. I have written on this subject in other books and have received many responses from readers who are going through the difficult and stressful process of divorce and have found the books a valuable resource to them.

It has been said that there are only two sure things in this world—death and taxes. If you were to examine the failure rate of marriages these days, however, you might believe that *divorce* will soon join that elite group. As mentioned above, one out of two marriages will end in divorce. One out of every two! I can't help but wonder how this situation got so out of control. In my opinion, there are basically two primary reasons for this sorry state of affairs, and they appear to be working in combination with each other. The first reason is spiritually related and the second is without question money-related.

According to all reports, the number one reason couples fight is *money*. We have all experienced stresses in our lives which are related to money, have we not? I would contend, though, that the issue is more complex than just arguing over a bad check or not having enough money to pay the babysitter. How exactly did we get to the point of constantly arguing about money? I believe that the ever-present rise in the cost of living, along with our government's insistence on imposing confiscatory tax rates (so that it may fund the plethora of social welfare programs it has implemented over the last 50 years) have much to do with it. Let's face it—it takes a lot more money to live than it used to.

What is the result? Well, one result is that we have less money to spend on the recreational activities which do so much to relieve our job-related stresses. We find ourselves tightening our belts to make do, and that tightening can make us feel quite uncomfortable. Another result which I believe to be very significant is that now, in most cases, both spouses must work in order to provide a decent standard of living for themselves and their children. With both husband and wife working, there is less time to devote to family matters. Furthermore, the workforce-related stresses are now doubled in the marriage.

I also believe that our society's emphasis on making things easier and faster, on providing instant gratification, shares much of the blame. We have become spoiled by the fact that so many daily chores and tasks have been greatly simplified or even completely eliminated. We are accustomed to not needing patience any longer. We want the answers to our problems quickly and without spending much effort. It is only natural, then, that we approach problems in our marriages with the same attitude. As couples we will simply have to commit to being more disciplined and to fight the temptation to look for easy answers if we are to reasonably expect this trend toward broken homes to reverse, or even slow, anytime soon.

For now, however, divorce remains a reality in American life. Although I had long wrestled with the question of whether it was appropriate for me to address the financial aspects of divorce (for fear I would be perceived as condoning the practice), I finally decided that to avoid doing so was impractical. Good Christian people, despite their efforts, are also frequent participants in divorce proceedings. Divorce raises a number of important issues; this chapter will try to deal effectively with some of the financial ones.

FREEDOM PRINCIPLE
If you are truly committed to the holy estate of matrimony, do not enter into a marriage with a prenuptial agreement.

How you view prenuptial agreements probably depends a lot on how you view marriage. If you believe that the institution of marriage is nothing special, or that divorce should be readily accepted as a necessary evil, you probably won't have much difficulty thinking that such agreements have their place in today's society. I have to disagree.

Do you recall what I said about being afraid of people thinking I condoned divorce? Well, I believe that if a person accepts the notion that prenuptial agreements are appropriate, then that same person must necessarily believe that divorce is an acceptable eventuality. I can't deny that prenuptial agreements can make good business sense for some people, but I reject the notion that a marriage should be viewed in the same way one would a merger of two companies. How close to his heart can a person truly hold the sanctity of marriage if that same person enters into it even considering the possibility of divorce? In the Bible, we find that God views marriage as a forever commitment: "For this cause a man shall leave his father and mother, and shall cleave to his wife; and the two shall become one flesh . . . They are no more two, but one flesh" (Matthew 19:5,6).

WHEN DIVORCE IS IMMINENT

If after every possible measure has been taken to avoid divorce you still do not see a way out, these next freedom principles will assist you in making the best of a bad situation.

FREEDOM PRINCIPLE
Notify all banks, credit card companies, and other similar financial institutions that you want your name removed from jointly held accounts, if you believe divorce is imminent.

From time to time I get questions on my radio show which revolve around what one spouse can do when the other spouse has run up the jointly owned credit cards to their limits. I have only one answer, and it's always the same: Pay the bills. Some of these listeners are shocked by my response, and I'm sorry for that. The truth is, however, that anything you jointly own you're each responsible for. The bank doesn't care about your personal problems, or about the fact that you knew nothing of the expenditures. The bank is simply concerned with getting its money. What's more, if these institutions can't locate both of the joint debtors, they are perfectly justified in trying to collect the full amount owed from one of the individuals.

These types of spending sprees are common when there is bitterness in a relationship. It may be a case of one spouse trying to destroy the other, or it may be the result of depression or emotional instability. Whatever the reason, see that you protect yourself. Once you have contacted each of these institutions by telephone to have them remove your name from these joint accounts, *follow up with a certified letter to these same institutions reiterating your wishes.* Do not get complacent about this. Debt problems will appear on your credit record, and they will do so (in this case) at about the time you'll need an A-1 credit rating the most.

FREEDOM PRINCIPLE
If you believe divorce is imminent, request copies of past tax returns from the IRS.

Although most married couples file their income tax jointly, it is typically only one spouse who completes the form, and it is usually that same spouse who does it year after year. If you are the spouse who doesn't really have much of a hand in these matters, you would be wise to secure copies of past years' tax returns. The purpose for doing this is to ensure that you are aware of all assets which exist in the marriage. Upon reviewing the returns, you may find evidence of a savings account which you never knew existed, or of a mutual fund account which up till now had been a well-kept secret. If you have a difficult time understanding the information contained on the forms, you may want to show them to a trusted adviser.

FREEDOM PRINCIPLE
Be sure your attorney subpoenas
the records of all accounts controlled
by your spouse.

This may seem a bit obvious, but I want you to watch out for something in particular: accounts in the names of your children for which your spouse serves as custodian. When I talked about Uniform Gifts to Minors Act (UGMA) accounts in the previous chapter, I briefly mentioned that some parents set up accounts like this simply to enjoy the tax advantages. There can be another reason, however: to store assets in the child's name, which can then be withdrawn after the divorce. Custodians of UGMA accounts have full authority to deposit and withdraw funds as they see fit. Although such transactions are supposed to be made out of deference to the best interests of the child, such requirements will not faze anyone who would engage in this type of manipulation to begin with.

FREEDOM PRINCIPLE
If your spouse owns a corporation,
be sure your attorney subpoenas the
tax returns of that entity.

Does your spouse own some type of business which is set up as a corporation? If you don't know for sure, find out. A corporation is a great place to hide assets; as long as the spouse controls the activities of the corporation, it doesn't really matter whether the Lexus he or she drives is owned by the person himself or by the corporation.

Be advised that you will not be able to obtain the copies of past corporate returns in the same way you were able to gain copies of your personal joint returns. The IRS won't send them to you simply at your request because the information they contain is, technically, none of your business. You will have to see to it that your attorney takes the necessary steps to subpoena the documents, which means that you'll have to know for sure that the corporate entity even exists. Do your homework.

FREEDOM PRINCIPLE
Ensure that the court takes steps to
determine whether your spouse is
hiding income at the workplace.

A common strategy used by primary wage-earners who are headed for divorce court is to make arrangements with the employer to hide income. The actual hiding is done in the form of income deferral, which means that the spouse has agreed to forsake a good portion of his salary until the divorce proceedings are complete. If the spouse also has the same ideas as you about where the marriage is going, it would be very easy for him or her to change his compensation structure. Of course the employer will probably be told that the deferral arrangements are being made for tax reasons, although he'll probably know the real reason. I can understand if you're reluctant to have the court investigate the possibility of this practice going on, but remember something: You may be in for the fight of your financial life.

FREEDOM PRINCIPLE
Begin to establish bank and credit card
accounts in your name only, as preparation for your eventual divorce.

As you see that your marriage is fast reaching the point of no return, you will have to begin giving some thought to what will happen once the legal proceedings are behind you. I would

DIVORCE

highly recommend that you take steps to develop a financial record of your own. If you happen to be the spouse who has never had many dealings with the family finances, or have never had even a credit card in your name alone, you have some work to do. See to it that you open both a checking and savings account, as well as begin to develop a credit record.

If you find that you're having a hard time being approved for an unsecured credit card, consider applying for a secured credit card. A secured credit card looks no different from any other Visa or MasterCard; the difference lies in the fact that your credit line is secured by a cash deposit you have made at the issuing bank. Typically, the amount of your deposit is equal to your credit limit, but the more progressive secured card issuers are now giving you a limit which is 150% of your deposit. I speak to many people who are reluctant to pursue the secured card option because they fear there's something on the card which will indicate that they are "different." That, however, is not the case. If you need to establish credit—and you will need to—a secured card may be your best option. Consult Appendix A for a list of secured card issuers.

FREEDOM PRINCIPLE
Take steps to prepare for
your own career.

If you are a spouse who has been out of the workforce for a long time, or perhaps have never really been a legitimate member of the workforce before in your life, you must think about how you will handle this situation once you are divorced. Think about what you might want to do for a living. Some people I speak to in this situation are quick to point out that they will be going back to school after they're divorced to earn a professional degree. I believe that's a great idea *if* you can do it. You will want to honestly assess your ability to go to school full-time once you're on your own. For many people, though, this is wishful thinking. My advice is to do what you can to ensure your survivability.

If you don't have that much time to prepare, my advice would be to take steps to secure part-time employment. Try to get a part-time job with an employer who can give you full-time hours once you are on your own. Don't be too prideful when looking for work; your primary concern at this point should be having the means to support yourself when the marriage dissolves. You may want to contact trusted friends who can assist you with your job search.

As the writer of this book I obviously cannot know if you are the one who will be receiving payment from your former spouse or the one paying it out. For this reason, listed below you will find a basic review of the tax consequences of payments of child support and/or alimony. I feel compelled to inform you of these facts, since many attorneys do not explain them to their clients. Without question these tax issues play an important role in any discussion of the financial aspects of divorce. I feel that this chapter would be incomplete without such an explanation.

FREEDOM PRINCIPLE
**If you are the primary wage-earner
and believe you will have to pay both
alimony and child support, you may want
to have more of what you must pay
classified as alimony.**

According to the IRS, alimony payments are tax-deductible to the spouse paying them. They are fully taxable, however, to the spouse receiving them. If you are the primary wage-earner in this relationship, it is likely that you will be required to pay alimony, child support, or both. If that in fact happens, it is to your advantage that what you pay to your ex-spouse be structured as alimony.

It should be noted that I am *not* encouraging you to maintain an adversarial relationship with your spouse/ex-spouse in this process. I am also in no way suggesting that you engage in any dishonest tactics during the course of these proceedings. My goal here is to inform you of the tax consequences to paying and receiving alimony, and to draw the conclusions which are quite logical and probably rather obvious.

FREEDOM PRINCIPLE
**If you are to be the recipient of alimony
and/or child support, you may want
to have more of what is paid to you
classified as child support.**

You might consider this to be the converse of the above principle. The payer of child support may not take any deduction for his payments. The recipient or payee, however, need not pay taxes on the money received as child support because the IRS has ruled that child support is not considered income. So if you are the spouse who expects to receive alimony and child support, you may want to try to have as much of the money as possible structured in the form of child support.

FREEDOM PRINCIPLE
**Construct (or reconstruct) a financial
profile on yourself after the divorce.**

Divorce is, of course, a life-changing experience. The plans and goals you had set for yourself may very well go up in smoke once that final split takes place. Besides, most of

DIVORCE

those goals were probably being worked toward jointly by you and your ex-spouse, so it's only natural that they would change for personal as well as economic reasons.

Your immediate strategy should be geared for self-preservation. If you are the ex-spouse who will be paying alimony and child support, you will want to account for these payments in the form of a monthly budget. Redo everything completely. I would advise that you do not reconfigure a monthly budget until the final arrangements are made and you know precisely what you will be paying for. If you are the ex-spouse who will be receiving alimony and child support, you will also want to account for the receipt of these monies in your monthly budget. The fact is that regardless of which ex-spouse you are, it's fair to say that your financial picture will change drastically following the divorce. In order that you stay on an even keel and know exactly where every dime is going, I strongly suggest that you complete a new budget worksheet. If you've never done one before, it's high time to start.

If the figure for disposable income is on the plus side, that represents how far ahead of your monthly obligations you are. If the figure is a negative, you must make immediate changes either in what you bring in or in what you pay out in order to eliminate that difference. Whether you actually see the effects yet or not, that negative figure does indicate that you are in debt.

DIVORCE

FREEDOM PRINCIPLE
If you are displaced after the divorce, rent
a home or apartment as soon as possible
so that you may begin building toward
the purchase of your own home.

A divorce usually results in one of two scenarios being played out as far as the family residence is concerned: Either

MONTHLY BUDGET STATEMENT

Monthly Income

Salary(ies) _____

Alimony _____

Child support _____

Other _____

TOTAL INCOME $_____

Monthly Expenses

Mortgage/rent _____

Food _____

Electricity _____

Telephone _____

Other utilities _____

Gas (for auto) _____

Life insurance _____

Health insurance _____

Auto insurance _____

Installment loans (auto, etc.) _____

Clothing _____

Laundry _____

Entertainment _____

Cable TV _____

Education _____

Credit cards _____

Miscellaneous/other _____

Monthly Tax-Deductible Expenses

Home loan interest _____

Child care _____

Alimony _____

Withholding taxes _____

Medical expenses _____

Charitable contributions _____

Miscellaneous/other _____

TOTAL EXPENSES _____

TOTAL INCOME _____

minus

TOTAL EXPENSES _____

equals

**TOTAL DISPOSABLE
   INCOME** _____

one spouse gets to keep the house while the other is required to leave, or the judge orders that the house be sold outright, forcing both ex-spouses to seek new living arrangements. Regardless of which circumstance it is, at least one and maybe both of you will have to find a new place to live.

After a divorce, you may be feeling depressed and somewhat alienated. The temptation to move in with a trusted friend or loved one for awhile may be strong, and that's understandable. However, if you plan on owning your own home again one day, you will want to participate in a lease-type arrangement which will help you build a record of making monthly payments to a landlord. This principle is especially important if you are the ex-spouse who had little involvement with financial affairs in the marriage, and maybe even had no assets held in your name whatsoever. Do your best to stay focused on your financial future.

FREEDOM PRINCIPLE
**If the divorce leaves you without a car,
simply concentrate on purchasing
what you can afford.**

I've noticed that cars can have a very intoxicating effect on people. Despite the many times I've spoken about what a lousy investment of your money a car represents, I continually encounter people who go out and purchase the top-of-the-line this or the top-of-the-line that. I've learned that there is a large segment of the population who refuse to view an automobile as simply a mechanism with which to travel from Point A to Point B. They've just *got* to look good getting there.

A divorce can leave you without a car in one of two ways. The first way is if the judge simply awards the car(s) to the other party. The other way is if the financial constraints placed on you by your alimony and child support obligations force you to give up the car you currently own. Do *not* risk jeopardizing your financial health by going out and purchasing a car you cannot afford. Now that you're on your own, you will certainly need a car; however, you would be well-advised to look at cars from the "Point A to Point B" perspective for awhile. There's no shame in driving a car which you believe is "beneath you." There can be dire consequences, however, to buying a car you cannot afford to pay for and maintain.

FREEDOM PRINCIPLE
**Build or rebuild a cash reserve for your-
self through small monthly contributions
to a no-load stock mutual fund.**

No matter on which side of the divorce you end up, there's a good chance that any cash resources or reserves you once had will be gone. Whether the money went to paying attorney's fees, honoring decreed obligations, or simply keeping your head above water doesn't matter; what matters is that you may not have a source of funds to fall back on if crises or emergency situations arise in the future. My advice is to begin building such a resource as soon as possible.

Refer back to the Monthly Budget Worksheet you completed earlier in the chapter. Focus on the figure you arrived at for disposable income. A good rule of thumb is to take one-third of that amount (assuming it's on the plus side, of course) and invest it in a no-load stock mutual fund on a monthly basis (see the information about dollar-cost averaging in Chapter 11).

Normally I do not recommend that someone build cash reserve with stock-based vehicles, but I am making an exception here because you probably will have very little to set aside each month—maybe $50. In order to reach your goal figure of three to six months' worth of living expenses in a timely fashion, you will have to avail yourself of the growth potential offered by the market. Besides, adding monthly to mutual funds (the dollar-cost averaging method) reduces your exposure to stock market volatility even further. I recommend that you use a somewhat conservative stock fund for these purposes.

As your reserve begins to take substantial shape, or as you find yourself able to make sizable contributions, you would be wise to transfer the funds to a money market vehicle so that every bit of it will be there should you need it.

FREEDOM PRINCIPLE
**Set up a retirement plan of your own if
you've been left without one.**

Depending upon your age and particular situation at the time of divorce, you may need to develop a retirement account of your own. If you did not have one at all, or saw the bulk of

DIVORCE

yours awarded to your ex-spouse in the divorce, you need to take steps to ensure that you won't have to rely solely on Social Security alone in your golden years.

Your first order of business is to build your cash reserve fund. Once that is in place, it's time to build a retirement fund. You could simply take the amount of money you've been setting aside each month for your cash reserve and continue to deposit it into a retirement account. The vehicle to use is an Individual Retirement Account, or IRA. IRAs can be set up at no-load mutual fund families, something which I heartily recommend that you do. If your job allows you to participate in an employer-sponsored retirement plan, I suggest that you pursue that option above all others.

FREEDOM PRINCIPLE
Ensure that you are covered by health insurance following the divorce.

You must pay close attention to what happens to your insurance coverage once you're divorced, particularly with regard to health coverage. If you were covered by your spouse's plan at work, that situation clearly doesn't exist any longer . . . or does it?

You *can* continue to remain on your spouse's plan for up to 36 months following the divorce, per the Congressional Omnibus Budget Reconciliation Act, or COBRA. You must be sure, however, to notify your ex-spouse's employer within 60 days of receipt of the notice which details this option. You should request this notice from your employer. If you are working somewhere that provides health coverage as a benefit, you may want to travel that avenue before enrolling in COBRA. Participation in COBRA will mean you have to pay group health rates, and they may not be cheap. See if your employer has a better deal. Besides, you can't stay on COBRA forever.

If participation in these group plans is not a viable option, then you will need another solution. Getting the kind of coverage offered by employer plans on an *individual* basis can be outrageously expensive. My recommendation is to shop around for the lowest-cost Major Medical coverage. Major Medical policies are designed to cover only the "big stuff"; they do not provide all the "bells and whistles" that the employer plans typically provide, but at least you're covered enough so that an accident or major illness doesn't wipe you out. A smart way to buy this type of coverage is with a $1000 deductible, which means that you're responsible for the first $1000 of medical expenses. That may seem like a lot, but remember that you are purchasing Major Medical so that you can walk the line successfully between having affordable coverage and having no coverage at all.

Though the emotional devastation caused by divorce can be irreparable, the financial devastation following a divorce can have similar effects. To avoid risking this kind of problem, it is up to *you* to ensure that your economic welfare is accounted for. No one else will be there to do it for you. Discipline yourself to become educated on all financial matters. It may very well mean the difference between living a miserable, bitter existence or one sustained by happiness and security.

The reason you have read this chapter may be that you have already decided there is no hope in your marriage. But I want to encourage you to keep trying, as we all know that God can work miracles. I highly recommend that you and your spouse tap into the many resources available for couples facing marital difficulty.

You'll also want to go to your local Christian bookstore and look for books that can help you and your spouse. You may also want to ask your pastor to recommend books that you could read or tapes that you could listen to. Whatever the final outcome of your circumstance, I sincerely hope that this chapter has given you some basic insight into how to make the best of a bad situation.

DIVORCE

11

PLANNING FOR RETIREMENT

My paternal grandparents were a great role model for how I would like to live in retirement. Once they retired, they had various recreational vehicles, everything from motor homes to camper trailers, and traveled the country from coast to coast. It would not be unusual at all for them to live somewhere for three or four months in one of their RVs and then pack everything up and find another place to live for a few weeks or months. The idea of having the freedom to pick up and go anywhere is very attractive to me. One of the first things I want to do during retirement is buy a motorhome and take a full year to travel the country with my wife.

Many people who retain me as their financial planner describe their retirement plans as "Someday I would like to have a nice retirement." The real challenge in retirement planning is to be as specific as you can so you can construct a plan to reach your actual retirement dreams. One of my clients described his retirement plan as having enough money to buy a mobile home and put it on a rented lot next to a lake. He said he would be happy if he had enough money to buy bait so he could fish every day. Retirement planning and retirement goals are as unique as the people who make them. For some people, their dream includes having two or three retirement homes, traveling the world, and funding their grandchildren's college education. For others the dream may be much more basic and modest. The key is to recognize that what we have belongs to God, so that as each of us plans our retirement, we recognize that our greatest retirement calling is to be a good steward of what God has given us.

PLANNING AHEAD: THE KEY TO SUCCESS

I have long believed, and will always believe, that the key to success in anything lies in the planning of it. Occasionally you may run across people who seem to be especially blessed financially, or have simply been the beneficiaries of good fortune, but counting on such windfalls of luck is no way to go about achieving our goals or realizing our dreams.

When it comes to working toward objectives which are financial in nature, I am a strong believer in using the financial planning approach. This approach involves designating a particular goal, determining how much time you want to take to reach the goal, and then determining how much money you need to set aside on a regular basis in order to meet that goal.

Of all the financial goals you may have, a secure retirement is probably the most suited for a financial planning approach. The reason is because retirement comes somewhat close to the end of your life. Therefore you should have the greatest amount of time to prepare for it. Yet the sad fact is that too many people allow the natural human inclination toward procrastination to get in the way of good planning. We have a tendency to put off dealing with what is not immediately facing us. When it comes to retirement, though, that can be a life-shattering mistake.

FREEDOM PRINCIPLE
The sooner you start planning, the better
retirement you'll have.

I cannot emphasize this enough: *Where retirement is concerned, the time to plan is now.* Although it's really never

RETIREMENT

too late to start planning, it is most certainly never too early. The difference is how much you will reasonably expect to have when the time comes for you to stop working permanently. Also, the earlier you start planning, the less you'll have to set aside on a regular basis to achieve your goal. The fact that the majority of older Americans retires in poverty is something I find heartbreaking and completely unnecessary. I constantly hear tales of older people who have become a burden to their children, who have had to sell their possessions, and who have even had to take to begging on the streets just to survive.

I still come across people who believe that Social Security will be the answer to their prayers. But I have news for you: The average monthly Social Security benefit is well under $700.00. In fact, Social Security was never intended to be more than a supplement in the first place. But there is even more ominous news about Social Security: It is estimated that by the year 2010 we will start to see real problems with the Social Security system. Why? Because the number of older Americans is growing so rapidly that not long after the turn of the century there won't be a working, taxpaying base sufficient in size to support them. Do you really believe you can count on this system to provide for you in your advanced years?

FREEDOM PRINCIPLE
**Buy a financial calculator to help you
with your retirement planning.**

If, after reading the chapter up to this point, you are committed to successfully planning your retirement, I suggest that you buy an inexpensive financial tool which will allow you to quantify and monitor your planning throughout the entire process. The tool I'm talking about is a financial calculator.

RETIREMENT

A financial calculator looks much like the typical pocket calculator we all know and love. The difference between the two is that the financial calculator has a few extra functions (keys) which allow you to account for the time value of money. The financial calculator allows you to answer such questions as "How much money do I need to set aside each month so that I will have $1,000,000 by the time I retire?" And that's a pretty good question. So let's see how we would go about answering it.

Before I start, let me say that I used a Radio Shack EC-5500 for this exercise. But any basic financial calculator would be appropriate, and they can be bought for under $30 at stores like Wal-Mart, K-Mart, Radio Shack, etc. Each financial calculator comes with an easy-to-read instruction booklet, so gaining quick familiarity with this device shouldn't be too difficult. Now let's move on to our problem.

Let's say you want to have $1,000,000 by the time you retire. Now at what age do you want to retire? 65? And how old are you currently? Based on these two ages, you want to have accumulated $1,000,000 by the end of the next 30 years. How much money have you saved so far? $1000? And what type of investment will you use to reach your goal? A certificate of deposit? That's fine, if that's what you really want to use, but now we need to pick an interest rate which the CD will likely earn on average over the next 30 years. Six percent sounds pretty good. Now we can turn to our calculators.

The basic functions we will use on the calculator are as follows:

PV	Present Value
FV	Future Value
N	Number of years or months
I	Interest rate
PMT	Monthly payment

Let's plug in the data we have already and see how much money we must deposit each month into that CD in order to reach our goal.

PV	1000
FV	1,000,000
N	360 (30 years multiplied by 12 months. Remember, we are seeking a *monthly* figure.)
I	.5 (6% interest divided by 12 months)

By tapping the "compute" key and then the "PMT" key, we'll know that $989.51 has to be set aside each month to reach the goal amount under these particular circumstances.

While having a financial calculator is by no means a requirement for you to realize success in your retirement planning, it enables you to project your financial needs and to implement your investment blueprint with greater accuracy. I recommend heartily that you go out and get one.

BUILDING YOUR NEST EGG

FREEDOM PRINCIPLE
For best results, look to stock mutual funds as an investment vehicle for retirement planning.

In the example we just went over with the financial calculator, I suggested that our generic investor would use a certificate of deposit as his investment vehicle of choice. Now while I named the CD simply for demonstration purposes, I hope you didn't miss something important—namely, that a

RETIREMENT

CD (or any other type of bank vehicle) is a very poor choice as a haven for your investment dollars. Do you see how much the investor in that example was going to have to put away *each month* for 30 years? Almost $1000! There is definitely a better way.

I think it's safe to say that all financial planners agree that for long-term investing, the stock market is the place to be. For the past 50 years or so, the stock market has returned an average of about 11% per year. Bear in mind that this 11% figure includes one of the worst economic collapses in modern times, as well as several recessions and periods of international conflict. Through it all, though, the stock market has been able to maintain an overall return in the double-digit range.

There is, however, some risk in trying to place your money with just a few individual companies. Many investors who buy individual stocks learn quickly how difficult it is to achieve even a minimal level of diversification. A stock that sells for $75 per share would create a transaction expense of over $7500 to purchase just 100 shares. It can be hard to spread out your money properly if you do not take a different approach. (The risk is obvious: If the fortunes of those companies you own shares in go sour, you may have very substantial losses which could wipe out your future financial plans and goals.)

The answer is to diversify your money across a great number of companies, and to have those selections made by an investment professional, a full-time stock market analyst. Where can you find this diversification and top-notch professional management? You can find it in a mutual fund. A mutual fund pools investors' money so that it can buy a portfolio of stocks. The number of stocks in just one mutual fund is typically between 50 and 200. What's more, the stock selections are made by a fund manager whose compensation is tied to the performance of the fund. As if this news isn't good enough, it gets better. You can actually invest in these stock mutual funds without paying a commission. *That* type of fund is referred to as a *no-load* (no-commission) mutual fund.

No-load mutual funds don't charge commissions because they're not sold by brokers or agents. Instead, they're advertised directly to the general public through the forum of mass media. The fund company makes its money by assessing a 1% (roughly) management fee on the assets under management, but because that fee is already calculated into the share price you don't really see it. At this time I should tell you that loaded mutual funds charge this management fee *in addition to* the load fee, which can cost as much as 8.5% of the money you want to invest. (Remember, the sole purpose of the load is to compensate the broker). Wouldn't you rather have the money for the load fee go toward your mutual fund investment rather than the pocket of a broker? For your convenience I have included a list of no-load mutual fund companies (called "families") in Appendix C.

FREEDOM PRINCIPLE
Create automatic wealth by using
the mutual fund company's
automatic investment plan.

Automatic investment plans have grown in popularity as America seems to get busier and busier every year. By filling out a simple form you can authorize the mutual fund company to automatically withdraw money from your checking account each month. By investing even a small amount of money each month (as low as $25 is acceptable at some companies) you can build a solid financial future. Investing systematically each month also takes advantage of an outstanding investment concept called "dollar cost averaging." This system of investing allows you to take much of the volatility out of the market because you are statistically buying at an *average* price over the

HOW DOLLAR COST AVERAGING WORKS

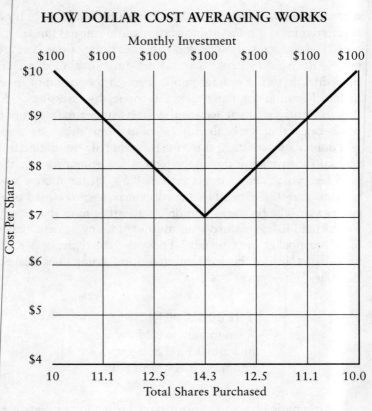

Monthly Investment

		Summary	Total
Average cost per share		8.59	$700
End value		10.00	$815
Profit		1.41	$115 or +16%

course of several months or years. Because you are not buying all at one time, your investment is being made during both up and down markets, thereby giving you an overall good value in terms of share price. By averaging into the market in this way you can avoid the disappointment of possibly getting in at a bad time.

Before I leave this discussion on stock mutual funds, I want to recalculate the exercise we did at the beginning, but this time I want to do so assuming that the investor chose no-load stock mutual funds as his retirement planning vehicle. Actually, to recalculate we need only change one figure—the assumed rate of interest. Let's assume that our investor will average 12% per year with mutual funds, which is very realistic. Remember, with CDs we assumed a rate of only 6%.

By recalculating with a 12% annual rate of return, we see that the investor need only deposit $275.84 per month in order to reach the goal, far less than the $989.51 originally figured with the certificate of deposit. Which do you think makes more sense?

FREEDOM PRINCIPLE
Make full use of your company
retirement plan.

If you are an employee of a company which has been in existence for at least a few years and is at least moderately sized, the chances are quite good that there is a retirement plan available for your participation which is sponsored by this company. Employers are finding that one of the best ways to secure loyalty from their employees is to provide them with the means to prepare for their retirement. There are different types of company-sponsored plans in existence, each named for the section of the Tax Code which names and defines it. The most common type of private company-sponsored retirement plan is known as a 401(K), or a salary reduction plan. Although salary reduction plans are known by different sections of the Tax Code, depending upon which type of employers sponsor them, we'll stick to the basic 401(K) for the sake of discussion.

A salary reduction plan works like this: Your employer holds back a percentage of your salary (usually up to about 10%) and puts that money into the account which has been set up in your name. The actual percentage amount set aside is dictated by you, and you can change the figure at any time. One desirable aspect of this plan is that it lowers the amount of income you report to the IRS each year, as you don't have to include for taxation the money you've allocated to your 401(K). A typical 401(K) will allow you to invest in a host of investment options, including stock mutual funds. If you have a long way to go until retirement, I suggest that you invest in more aggressive stock mutual funds. If you have less time available (less than 10 years), you might want to allocate a sizable portion of your money into more conservative stock mutual funds.

A couple of additional things need to be said about these plans, one good and one not so good. First, find out if your employer will match or at least partially match your monthly contribution. Many employers will contribute, say, 50 cents for every dollar you contribute. This means that before your investments have even begun to perform, you are making a 50% return on your money! The not-so-good feature is a limited number of investment choices in some plans. Not all 401(K)s are created the same. Some offer numerous high-quality mutual funds, while others offer very poor choices.

I ran across a 401(K) one time which actually offered only a bond mutual fund and a money market fund as the choices to employees—no stocks at all. The returns on stocks can be as much as three times that of a money market fund and often double that of a bond fund (of course this varies based on market conditions). If you have the kind of 401(K) where sizable employer contributions exist, you may want to stick with it even though the investment choices are limited.

However, if your 401(K) does not have employer contributions as a feature, and the choices are also quite limited, you might be wise to forgo the 401(K) and instead set up an Individual Retirement Account.

FREEDOM PRINCIPLE
**Maintain an Individual Retirement
Account whenever possible.**

The company-sponsored retirement plan probably represents your best bet for achieving a successful retirement. However, if you do not work for a company which offers any type of retirement plan, or only have access to one which offers substandard investment choices, you have another option: The Individual Retirement Account or IRA.

An IRA is sometimes a source of confusion, as many Americans believe that an IRA is itself some particular type of investment. Instead, an IRA is actually just a tax-deferred "umbrella" under which you may put just about any type of investment: stocks, bonds, mutual funds, certificates of deposit, etc. It is this flexibility which makes IRAs the preferred choice of so many Americans.

The existence of the IRA was authorized years ago by a government which rightfully became concerned about the large number of its citizens who appeared headed for no haven besides the social welfare rolls. As a result, Americans may now deposit up to $2000 per year of earned income into an IRA ($250 per year for a nonworking spouse under present law) and see this money grow tax-deferred, which means that it grows tax-free until it is withdrawn by the retiree. The idea is that the years of tax-free compounding will much more than offset the tax liability incurred when the money is eventually taken out. For your information, IRA money may not be withdrawn without an IRA penalty before age 59 1/2 (with a certain few exceptions), and you *must* begin withdrawing no later than age 70 1/2.

RETIREMENT

Another feature of an IRA is that your annual contribution may be tax-deductible. If neither you nor your spouse is covered by a company-sponsored retirement plan, you may both fully deduct your IRA contributions. If you are single and make $25,000 or less per year, or are married and jointly make $40,000 or less per year, you may fully deduct your IRA contribution(s) even if you or your spouse is covered by a company plan. If you are single and make at least $35,000 per year, you may not deduct any of your IRA contribution. If you are married and jointly make at least $50,000, you also may not deduct any of your contribution.

If your income falls within the ranges outlined here, you will be able to deduct some portion of your contribution. If you are single, you lose $200 of your deduction for every $1000 of income you earn over $25,000. If you are married, you lose $200 of your deduction for every $1000 of income you earn over $40,000. Remember, all of these special rules apply only to IRA investors who are *also* covered by a company-sponsored retirement plan. If you are *not* covered by such a plan, you may fully deduct your annual contribution each year regardless of how much money you earn.

FREEDOM PRINCIPLE
Contribute to an IRA even if you
are not entitled to take a tax
deduction for doing so.

Even if you cannot deduct one dime of your annual IRA contribution, you should still have a nondeductible IRA. In my opinion, too many people evaluate the IRA's usefulness on the basis of whether or not their contribution is tax-deductible. That's a nice feature to have, but the real benefit is found in the tax-deferred growth of the investments you place within the IRA. Remember, you can set up your IRA almost anywhere. I suggest you set it up anywhere which will allow you to invest in no-load mutual funds. Most of the no-load mutual fund families located in Appendix C will act as the trustee of your IRA for a very nominal fee (from zero to $25 per year). The reason you need a trustee is that the IRS requires that these funds be held by an approved company so that all IRS reporting requirements are met.

FREEDOM PRINCIPLE
**Invest any additional monies you have
available for retirement investing
into a variable annuity.**

Let's say you've "maxed out" your company-sponsored retirement plan as well as your Individual Retirement Account, but you still have more money to invest. Where do you go? My advice is to place that money in a variable annuity. "That sounds great," you might say, "but I have just one question: What in the world is a variable annuity?"

To understand a variable annuity, you'll need to know about the annuity concept in general. For years there was only one type of annuity available—a fixed annuity. With a fixed annuity, you give your money to an insurance company, which then agrees to pay you a stated rate of interest. This rate of interest is usually very close to that available in bank CDs. However, annuities grow tax-deferred, just like IRAs and company retirement plans. Also, as with IRAs and company retirement plans, annuities may not be accessed before age 59 1/2 without a penalty (again, with a certain few exceptions). The original idea behind the annuity was that you give your money to a life insurance company, they invest it for growth, and you receive a monthly income from that insurance company once you retire. The process by which you signal the insurance company to start sending you your monthly income is called "annuitizing."

RETIREMENT

The variable annuity, also available from an insurance company, works a bit differently. With a variable annuity you have the ability to invest your money in a variety of options, including stock mutual funds. If the variable annuity which you invest in has a competitive selection of fund options, you could easily find yourself making a double-digit rate of return over a period of several years.

I'm against choosing a *fixed* annuity for your investment money for a couple of reasons. First, the money you put in a fixed annuity becomes part of the assets of the life insurance company. If the company runs into financial difficulty, you could lose your investment. Also, I'm against investing in fixed annuities for the same reason I'm against investing your IRA in a bank CD: The return is quite poor. Whenever you have the option of investing in stock mutual funds for long periods of time, take it.

Here are a few more things you should know. Because you fund an annuity with after-tax dollars, your deposits are not tax-deductible. Also, many (though not all) variable annuities assess deferred sales charges if you move out of the annuity within the first five or six years of owning it. Finally, never "annuitize" the account. Remember, annuitizing means that the insurance company keeps your investment and pays you a monthly sum which is based on its own tables. Insurance companies get rich by paying annuity distributions to investors with internal rates of return of only 3% to 5%.

Also, if you die and do not have a survivor provision in your agreement, the company keeps all the remaining money. If, however, you choose the survivor option, so that your spouse continues to receive the payments after you death, the insurance company still wins. They simply penalize you for choosing this option by reducing your monthly payment. Once you are ready to retire, it is far better to withdraw the entire amount in a lump sum and invest it in mutual funds.

RETIREMENT

THE POWER PYRAMID OF RETIREMENT PLANNING

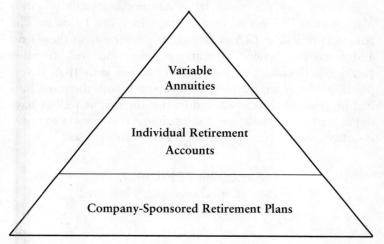

Variable
Annuities

Individual Retirement
Accounts

Company-Sponsored Retirement Plans

FREEDOM PRINCIPLE
Structure your retirement investing in accordance with the Power Pyramid of Retirement Planning.

To ensure that your retirement investments are placed as wisely as possible, I highly encourage you to invest in accordance with the Pyramid detailed above. Always start by making sure you are participating as fully as possible in your company-sponsored retirement plan. Once you have met that standard, go on to set up an Individual Retirement Account. Remember, don't get bogged down in determining whether or not your contribution is deductible; the benefit of the IRA lies in the tax-deferral. If, after utilizing both the company plan and the IRA, you still have some funds remaining to invest,

RETIREMENT

then make one more step up the Pyramid to the variable annuity.

By the way, don't ever let an annuity agent talk you into placing your IRA *inside* an annuity, which can be done. The reason is this: The IRA is already tax-deferred, so there's no additional tax benefit to you for doing this. Additionally, you'll lose flexibility as far as where to put your IRA; if you put it inside an annuity, you're now stuck with the more limited investment choices offered by the annuity, as well as having to deal with the deferred sales charge if you want to move it out within the first five or six years (in most cases).

FREEDOM PRINCIPLE
Stay clear of insurance which is geared
specifically toward the elderly.

We've all seen them: the television ads featuring a well-known celebrity who pushes special insurance designed for older Americans. You can buy health coverage which "picks up where Medicare leaves off" as well as life insurance which costs "less than a dollar a week." Why am I against purchasing this type of insurance? Simple: It is very overpriced. If you were to carefully evaluate how much insurance coverage you're really getting for what you're paying, you would find that the "great deals" are really nothing but rip-offs.

Take the life insurance, for example. One of the hallmarks of these plans is that they guarantee you won't be turned down for coverage, that you don't have to provide evidence of insurability. Now, wait a minute. Knowing that the likelihood of dying increases as you get older, what insurance company in its right mind would make available dirt-cheap coverage and also make it available to anyone, regardless of his or her health? The fact is that you typically receive a very

RETIREMENT

small amount of coverage, and there can be several restrictions within the terms of the policy which will make collecting difficult (this aspect applies even more to the similarly advertised health policies).

I believe that a great resource for people who are at or near retirement age is the American Association of Retired Persons, or AARP. AARP is a huge trade association which acts primarily in the capacity of consumer advocate for the elderly. AARP can assist you with questions about the kinds of insurance programs we've just discussed, as well as with many other issues which pertain to older Americans. To find out more about joining AARP, call 202-434-2277.

FREEDOM PRINCIPLE
**You know your retirement planning has
been successful when you can achieve
financial independence.**

The goal of retirement planning is that one day you'll be able to cease working altogether and still maintain the lifestyle to which you've become accustomed. Your planning can really be considered successful only when you've reached that point. To enhance that probability of success, you must use all the planning options at your disposal. Furthermore, I would encourage you once again to buy a financial calculator, for it will allow you to monitor your progress through the years. By "running the numbers," you'll find out if you need to contribute more to your plans in order to reach success, or even if you can get away with putting in less.

NEVER TOO LATE

This brings me to an important point. Although I believe the definition of successful retirement planning lies in your ability

RETIREMENT

to live financially independent, I must tell you that it is never too late to do something. I suppose if you've waited all the way up to the actual point of retirement before doing anything, then you probably won't be able to accomplish much, but that's not the scenario I'm referring to. I'm talking about someone who is maybe 55 years old and has done very little by way of investing. Typically, people who fit that profile despair that it is too late for them to help themselves.

Not true! Remember, a 55-year-old person has ten years to go before he reaches the generally accepted age of retirement. Spending ten years in a high-quality growth mutual fund can bring significant results to someone who has the dedication to making the investment in the first place. Although financial independence is my definition of successful planning, you should at least strive to accumulate as much money as possible for your golden years, no matter how much or how little that ends up being.

FREEDOM PRINCIPLE
Don't feel that you must retire.

The fact is that Americans are living longer and healthier lives. The trend in the last 20 to 30 years toward eating better and exercising more is having a profound effect, as are the advances in medicine which seem to be made almost daily. One of the chief results of all of this is that many people are becoming increasingly reluctant to stop working completely, as they find themselves every bit as physically and mentally capable as ever.

I share their reluctance. God willing, I see no reason why I can't continue writing books, giving lectures, and appearing on radio and television into my seventies and eighties. Stories abound of people who loved to work but were forced to retire, then died a short time later. When someone is happy at work, that happiness is reflected throughout every aspect of that person's life. Plan for your retirement thoughtfully and with foresight, but ultimately look at the retirement decision as an option, not a requirement.

If you're forced to retire due to age restrictions (and those rules are changing all the time, too), plan for that in advance by investigating the possibility of setting up your own small business. Consult your local bookstore for the many fine handbooks that are now available which give instructions on how to set up a small business.

RETIREMENT

WHAT TO LEAVE
YOUR LOVED ONES

Over the past several years, the most difficult part of my position as a financial planner is being called upon to counsel a person who has recently lost his or her spouse. In one sense we all accept the certainty of death, and we also understand that in most cases it will be an unpredictable event. Having this intellectual understanding that all of us will one day leave this earth should cause us to be motivated to leave our family with a solid estate plan. Very important issues must be decided—not only who will receive your assets, and in what amount, but also who would become the guardian of your minor children. Though most of us may never come to grips totally with our mortality, this chapter will help us to see the benefit of leaving a legacy for our family rather than financial chaos upon our death.

How do you feel today? Healthy, strong, full of life? Maybe you're on the company softball team, or perhaps you lift weights three days a week. Are you one of those people who meticulously eyes everything he eats to ensure that only low-fat, high-fiber foods pass his lips? If so, I have a news flash for you: You're going to die anyway. I don't say this to try to talk you out of taking good care of yourself while you're here; I only say it to help convince you that no matter what you do, no matter how well you live, someday you will be here no more.

The startling fact is that only one-third of all Americans have done even the most basic level of estate planning: written a will. Estate planning is the process of arranging your personal affairs so that upon your death, the "assets" (children, money, property) you leave behind are disposed of in accordance with your wishes.

Many estate-planning professionals have come to the conclusion that part of the reason so few people maintain a will is related to their refusal to accept the eventuality of death. I know this sounds childish, but it's true. Yet, here's a sobering thought to consider: What if you don't live a long, natural life? What if a serious accident or illness befalls you well before you're ready to go? These things *do* happen. You might not die for another 40 years; but you also might die tomorrow. If this happens to you, will your family be cared for properly? Will your money and other assets be distributed in accordance with your wishes? If you don't even have a will, you can be sure of nothing.

FREEDOM PRINCIPLE
**Everyone, regardless of net worth,
should have a will.**

Although fear of dying is a common reason why most people don't maintain wills, there are other common reasons as well. The first of these is that many people believe they don't have enough assets to warrant constructing a will. The second reason is that many people think their estates will simply take care of themselves. But they're wrong on both counts. The reason these assumptions are both wrong and dangerous has to do with one thing: *probate*.

When you die without a will, it is called *dying intestate*. When you die intestate, your estate is thrown into probate court to be settled. Think of probate as estate planning for

ESTATE PLANNING

those who didn't do any estate planning. The problem is that with *this* kind of estate planning, a judge will make all the decisions for you that you should have made for yourself and your family. Do you know this judge? How can you be sure that the decisions he makes are in agreement with what you would like to see happen? For the loved ones left behind who must endure the whole thing, probate will be an agonizing ordeal. I suppose if you truly own *nothing* of value, and have absolutely *no* heirs, dying without a will may not be such a crisis. However, how many people can honestly say that these two unique features apply to them?

Up to this point I've taken for granted the idea that everyone knows what a will is. Just to be sure, let's go over it. A will is nothing more than written instructions from you on how your assets should be disposed of at the event of your death. Your will should also account for what you would like to see happen to your children, if that may reasonably become a question; if you're married, think of the mess that may result if both you and your spouse die at the same time and there's no will to be referred to. To be considered valid, in most states, a will should be witnessed by two or three people who have no relation to you or your estate. Additionally, you will want to choose an executor for your estate along with the will. The executor's job is to see that the wishes you have outlined in the will are actually carried out. Your executor should be someone with at least a working knowledge of financial matters, preferably a close friend or relative.

I want you to know that a will also enters the probate process, but the reason in this case is simply to determine the legality and authenticity of the instrument rather than to decide how your assets are to be disposed of (that's why you wrote the will in the first place). The probate process is much quicker and cleaner when you have a will because you've left nothing up to interpretation.

ESTATE PLANNING

FREEDOM PRINCIPLE
If you want to see specific people inherit
particular tangible assets of yours,
place a Tangible Personal Property
Memorandum in your will.

If you know that a certain item you own may be near and
dear to the heart of a loved one, you might want to ensure that
the item in question passes right to the beneficiary without any
difficulty. To do this, simply designate a special provision in
your will known as a Tangible Personal Property Memorandum. This should take care of such special bequests (your
attorney will be able to advise you further on this).

FREEDOM PRINCIPLE
Whenever possible, use the services of an
attorney when constructing a will.

A will can be a simple document, but it is always a *legal*
document. While there are many do-it-yourself will kits available
in the marketplace these days, I must recommend that you consult an attorney for your will preparation needs. The disposition
of your estate is just too important a matter to deal with other
than with the highest level of expertise and completeness. If you
believe that the resolution of your estate may be at all complex,
then you should absolutely use the services of an attorney.

Although for most wills it is best to go to an attorney
who specializes in the area of estate planning, any attorney
would probably be sufficient for the purpose of putting
together a relatively simple will. Yes, the fee will probably be
about $100 to $200 but this is not an area where you should
cut corners. Your state bar association can give you a referral
for an estate planning attorney in your area, or you can
contact the leading trade association for such lawyers, the

ESTATE PLANNING

American College of Trust and Estate Counsel. This group can be reached by calling 310-398-1888.

FREEDOM PRINCIPLE
**A do-it-yourself will is always
better than no will at all.**

I hope you are convinced by now of the importance in having a will drafted. I guess if you're *not* a believer now, then you never will be, and that's too bad (particularly for those you leave behind). I believe that to do it right and to leave nothing to chance, it is best that you engage the services of an attorney. If, for whatever reason, you don't get around to consulting with an attorney, you still need to take care of these matters.

I mentioned before that there are do-it-yourself will kits available these days. Most bookstores carry them, and they are actually quite easy to implement. To be honest, you should have little trouble getting by with a do-it-yourself will kit as long as you don't have a lot of assets, and the disposition of what you *do* have is simple and straightforward. Remember, don't get caught without a will. If you feel you may not take the trouble to consult with an attorney, you can call my organization at 1-800-877-2022 and purchase a do-it-yourself will kit for $19.95. The process of completing a do-it-yourself will is not difficult, and it will give you and your family the peace of mind knowing that the processing of your estate will not be in the hands of a stranger.

FREEDOM PRINCIPLE
**Consider the fairness of the stipulations in
your will if you want to be sure your
estate is not the subject of future discord.**

Although a will is something everyone should have, it is nevertheless a document of tremendous importance. The writing

ESTATE PLANNING

of the will is a huge responsibility and should not be taken lightly. Before you actually put the document together, be sure you are accounting for all assets as well as all rightful heirs. Do not presume that a person who considers himself to be a legitimate heir to your estate will simply go and crawl underneath a rock if he finds that there's nothing going to him. He may very well challenge, or contest, the will. If you believe that such a course of action may be a possibility in your case, take some time to rethink the wisdom of the bequests found in your will. Reconsider all the heirs mentioned in the will to ensure that you are not leaving someone out.

Money, as we all know, can have a very divisive effect on families when one member of the family perceives that he did not get his fair share. If such a person is particularly bitter, he can initiate a challenge to the document. This is another reason why it is so important that your will be as intelligently and as professionally designed as possible; you want to limit as much as possible the opportunity for some angry relative (whom you probably never liked anyway) to throw a monkey wrench in the disposition process on the basis of some careless loophole. Use a big chunk of foresight when deciding how your possessions will be split up.

FREEDOM PRINCIPLE
Review your will regularly to ensure
that it accurately reflects your current
wishes and circumstances.

Although the task of drafting your will may be complete, you can't simply put the document away and forget about it, at least not completely. I would suggest that, in the absence of any major changes to your lifestyle or asset base, you review your will at least once a year. By doing so you can be sure your wishes as reflected in the will haven't changed.

ESTATE PLANNING

If you *do* experience significant changes in your asset base or lifestyle which need to be accounted for in the will, make those changes as soon as possible. One of the most common reasons for changing a will is divorce. A spouse is no longer a spouse, and therefore usually no longer an heir after the divorce decree. Don't get complacent about these kinds of things. It's very easy to put off making these necessary changes; if you do, however, you run the very serious risk of having your estate (or part of it, anyway) end up in the hands of the wrong person.

The easiest way to facilitate a change to the will is with the use of a codicil. A codicil is simply an amendment to the document which indicates the change to be made. It is especially important when adding a codicil that you sign and date it, thereby indicating without question that the document is in fact an amendment created *after* the original document. The codicil should also be witnessed as in the original will document.

FREEDOM PRINCIPLE
**If your net worth is greater than
$600,000, establish a living trust to
help reduce estate taxes.**

The federal government grants each person an exemption of up to $600,000 on estate taxes. It's fortunate that they do this, because the taxes they apply to amounts *beyond* the $600,000 amount border on highway robbery. A legitimate way to shelter more than the initial $600,000 from estate taxes is through the use of a living trust.

A living trust, as the name implies, allows you to place your assets into a trust while you are still alive. Typically, you would name yourself as the trustee while you are still alive, but would also make some provisions for a co-trustee or successor trustee to take control if you are incapacitated.

ESTATE PLANNING

Although the primary reason to set up a living trust is to reduce estate taxes, there are many other good reasons why someone might want to have a living trust. First, a living trust avoids probate, which is a significant benefit. Remember the potential misery which can result from loved ones having to deal with probate court? A living trust short-circuits that whole mess. Additionally, setting up a living trust allows conservatorship to be avoided. Again, and perhaps most importantly (for some people), a living trust can be constructed in such a way that a married couple may unify their $600,000 apiece estate tax exemptions. The result is a "his and hers" or A/B trust, which can shelter up to $1,200,000 from the confiscatory estate tax menace.

If you decide that a living trust would be a good idea for you, contact an estate planning attorney to help you with the arrangements. As with a will, it is always a good idea to consult with a professional whenever you are drawing up an important legal document. However, if you decide you definitely want the living trust but just can't seem to make it in front of an attorney, feel encouraged to purchase a do-it-yourself living trust kit from my organization. You may do so by calling 1-800-877-2022. The cost of the kit is $19.95.

I realize that many of you may not have a very good idea as to what your net worth is, so you may not have any notion as to whether or not you might need a living trust. If you take a few minutes to fill out the following information, you'll not only know whether you can benefit (from a tax standpoint) by setting up a trust, but you'll also know for general purposes what you're worth. For those of you who don't know what net worth is, it's simply the figure which results when you subtract your liabilities from your assets.

You should know that one skill any insurance agent worth his salt must possess is the ability to sell big insurance policies to people to pay the inheritance taxes for their heirs. Generally, people with estates over $600,000 (or, with the use

NET WORTH STATEMENT

1. Liquid assets   _____
    Checking accounts   _____
    Savings accounts   _____
    Certificates of deposit   _____
    Money market accounts   _____
    Treasury Notes   _____
    Cash on hand   _____
    Other   _____

2. Negotiable securities (non-retirement)   _____
    Stocks   _____
    Bonds   _____
    Mutual funds   _____
    Other   _____

3. Retirement plans
    Company-sponsored   _____
    IRAs   _____
    Annuities   _____

4. Life insurance   _____
    Cash value   _____

5. Real Estate   _____
    Residence   _____
    Other home   _____
    Rental property   _____

6. Personal property   _____
    Antiques   _____
    Furnishings   _____
    Appliances   _____
    Autos   _____
    Boats   _____
    Other vehicles   _____
    Computers   _____
    Clothing   _____
    Jewelry   _____

ESTATE PLANNING

Net Worth Statement continued

Tools   _____

         TVs, VCRs, etc.   _____

         Other   _____

TOTAL ASSETS $_____

         Liabilities

1. Mortage loans   _____

      Primary residence   _____

      Other homes   _____

      Rental property   _____

2. Installment loans   _____

      Automobiles   _____

      Furniture   _____

      Appliances   _____

      Other   _____

3. Miscellaneous loans   _____

      Unsecured (credit cards)   _____

      Other   _____

TOTAL LIABILITIES $_____

ESTATE PLANNING

_____   —   _____   = $_____

Total Assets   Total Liabilities   Current Net Worth

Now you have just calculated your current net worth. To determine your net worth at the event of your death, you must account for the death benefit (the cash-accumulated value) of your life insurance policies, which will obviously be paid at that time. Do it now.

_____ + _____ — _____ = $_____

Current Net   Face Value of   Cash Value of   Current Net Worth

Worth   Life Insurance   Life Insurance   Value at the Event

                                                     of Your Death

of a living trust, $1,200,000) are subject to federal and state estate taxes. If you are a really great parent (as your kids might say), you will leave your estate primarily to your children. If you are a really, really great parent, you will also pay the taxes on the estate so your heirs inherit the assets tax-free! Some of the clients I have worked with were leaving their children millions and felt guilty that their children would have to pay taxes on the money! This is like the game show winner expecting to take all his winnings and have the taxes paid for on top of it!

I will probably not settle the argument here about whether a parent should pay the estate taxes for his or her children, so let's deal with the fundamental problem instead, which is a myth about insurance. There is no way that it makes sense to buy life insurance when a person is older than 60 for the purpose of paying estate taxes. Should we really believe that the insurance company doesn't know we are going to die within 20 to 25 years? Do we believe that the least expensive way to pay these expenses is to pay the insurance company first and then they will pay our estate taxes for us? For the sake of simplicity, let's not call it estate taxes but just think of it as a future bill that will be due upon your death. Let's also assume that you have decided that this bill will be $1,000,000. To get the insurance company to pay your bill, you will statistically pay out at least three to five times the million in premiums and lose the time value of your money in the process.

FREEDOM PRINCIPLE
**Use the annual gift exclusion to
reduce the value of your estate
during your lifetime.**

I don't know if you realize this, but you may give a certain amount of your money away each year without having to pay a gift tax. The law says that you may give up to $10,000 to someone each year, and that someone does not even have to be a relative. If you are married, you and your spouse can combine your exclusions and give away $20,000 per recipient per year. The effectiveness of this Principle should be readily apparent. By doing nothing more complicated than giving your money away while you are alive to the people who will eventually be your heirs anyway, you could significantly reduce the size of your estate. If you have two children, you and your spouse could give each of them $20,000 per year, for an annual total of $40,000. Do that for three years, and you've now reduced the size of your estate by $120,000.

I do want to say that while I believe the annual gift exclusion can be a helpful estate planning tool, I would be wary of relying on it wholly as an estate planning mechanism. For one thing, there may not be that many people available to whom you feel comfortable gifting your money. For another, unless you know your death is imminent, you can't be sure how much money you'll need to live on for the future. Furthermore, if your estate is worth a fortune, chances are that this little device won't be terribly helpful anyway. Know that the exclusion exists, but use it wisely.

FREEDOM PRINCIPLE
Establish a Charitable Remainder Trust
to give money to your favorite charity
at the event of your death.

This is a great way to donate money to your favorite charitable organization. With this type of trust you may deposit an unlimited amount of assets into the trust, assets which are then excluded from your estate for federal tax purposes. The beauty of a Charitable Remainder Trust lies in the fact that you may also derive an income from the assets while you're still alive. For example, let's say you place highly valued stocks or mutual funds into the trust. Up to the time of your death, you may receive a monthly income and remain in control of the trust which is generated by these assets. When you die, the remaining assets in the trust pass directly to the charitable organization. You should also know that you get to take an immediate tax deduction for your contribution, although this is limited to some extent by Treasury Regulations. To find out more about setting up this type of trust, consult an estate planning attorney.

Although I have so far focused exclusively on matters relating to disposition of assets, there is more than that to estate planning. Estate planning also involves the preparation for what exactly will happen to *you* at the time of your death. I realize that this area of planning can be difficult to deal with, but always keep your loved ones in mind. Remember, they're the ones who will have to contend with the shock and grief which will follow your passing. One of the most caring, most loving actions you can take is to map out exactly what you'd like to have happen at and around the event of your death.

FREEDOM PRINCIPLE
**Ensure that you have a living will if
you don't wish to have your life
artificially sustained.**

Medical science never ceases to amaze me. It seems that I'm hearing about one great breakthrough after another almost daily. There is, however, a "miracle" of modern medicine which is not always highly regarded by everyone: artificial life support. This kind of support is the conglomeration of feeding tubes, pumps, and other apparatus which doctors can use to keep you alive when the ability for you to do that on your own seems hopeless. Many people believe that life support is simply a way of postponing the inevitable, while others

ESTATE PLANNING

disagree with its use on the basis that it interferes with the will of God (although I've heard some say its use permits the opportunity for a miracle to occur). Still others shy away from life support simply because they don't wish to prolong the misery and false expectations of family members.

Whatever your reasons are for not wanting to have life support used on your behalf, you may wish to have that desire formally noted in a living will. A living will is a legal document which declares that you do not wish to have your life sustained through artificial means, and permits doctors and relatives to disconnect any such equipment. Almost all states seem to recognize the right to die, but you will definitely need to put your desires in writing to ensure that they are carried out. It's not enough to simply tell your spouse or other loved one to see that such means are not implemented; a doctor, whose job it is to sustain life, will not abide by such hearsay information. The living will must be in *written* form, and it should be constructed by an estate planning attorney.

FREEDOM PRINCIPLE
Prearrange your funeral and burial
to spare your loved ones
additional heartaches.

Remember what I said: When you're dead, your earthly responsibilities are finished. However, it's your loved ones who must go through the dreaded process of arranging your funeral. If you would like to help them avoid that process almost entirely, why don't you pre-arrange your own funeral and burial? First of all, you will most certainly get a better deal on price because there is no immediate need for the services. Although it may seem a but morbid, you should shop around for this service like you would any other. Another benefit is that you will be able to plan your own funeral and burial in exact accordance with your wishes.

Be aware of a few things when shopping around for such programs. First, ensure that what you pay now will be sufficient to cover your funeral 30 years from now. In other words, be certain that you are protected against future price increases. Also, see to it that a refund clause is structured in the agreement so that if you have a change of heart, you can get your money back (within a reasonable period of time). One more thing: Be sure you know precisely with whom your contract is made. If it is with a general service which can be used anywhere, that's one thing. If, however, it is with a specific funeral home, find out what happens to you and your money if the day of your death comes and that home is no longer in business.

We've talked about several issues in this chapter, and I know they haven't all been pleasant. I do hope, though, that you realize how tough resolving a poorly planned estate can be for the loved ones you leave behind. Take some time to think about how much each of them truly means to you, and then decide if there's any way you can improve on the planning you may have already done. Total, loving estate planning can be the greatest gift you will ever give to those you love most of all.

ESTATE PLANNING

TEN STEPS TO FINANCIAL FREEDOM

If you've made it this far, perhaps you're thinking, "I've learned a lot of great things, but now where do I go? What do I do? How do I apply what I've learned to my own situation?" Good questions, since learning new financial concepts and strategies won't do you much good if you can't actually implement them in your daily life. The purpose of this section is to show you how to apply much of what you've learned.

It is a known fact that, on average, people spend more time planning their vacations each year than they do their retirement. It is probably fair to say also that most people don't spend much time engaging in financial planning of *any* type.

What are the reasons for this? First and foremost, lifetime financial goals are usually long-term in nature, which means that we find them easy to put off planning for. Most of us tend to procrastinate, to keep putting off until tomorrow what we could be doing today. If something isn't immediately relevant, we find it too abstract to consider. Our daily lives are full of hustle and bustle, and it seems as though that situation worsens with each passing year. As soon as some new gadget or gizmo is invented to help us free up more time, we find another "today task" to fill up that freed-up time.

Let's say you find an additional hour in your day today, for whatever reason (canceled doctor's appointment, *anything*).

Let's also suppose you've been wanting to go down to the local video rental store and pick up a new release. Now, how do you think you'll fill that 60-minute gap? Will you sit down and call some mutual fund families to receive information on setting up the retirement plan you don't have, or will you run down to the video store? Will you call an insurance company to inquire about term life insurance coverage and how it can save you money, or will you race down to rent the movie? Think about your priorities in the light of your long-term future.

Another reason people avoid financial planning is because they find it boring. I will be the first to admit that the words "financial planning" and "excitement" aren't exactly synonymous, but is it realistic to avoid any activity which doesn't provide you with a laugh a minute or the thrills of a hockey game? Maybe you consider financial planning to be too reminiscent of the homework you hated in high school, the same homework which kept you inside when you wanted to be out socializing. But now you're an adult, and where financial planning is concerned, the stakes are even higher than in high school.

Still another reason many people steer clear of planning is that they believe it to be too complicated. However, in my years of experience in helping people manage their finances, only a few people have a truly complex financial or legal situation. I would hope that, after reading this book, you can see for yourself that basic financial planning concepts and techniques are relatively easy to understand and implement.

Finally, many people shy away from sound financial planning because it requires discipline. If you have a long-term goal, the only way of realistically meeting it is through a disciplined approach. Once you know, for example, how much money you have to deposit each month to retire with your goal figure achieved, you must maintain the discipline necessary which allows you to stick with that essential habit. If you want to be sure you don't get caught up in paying off too much credit card debt, you need to avoid using your cards for purposes other than what I have recommended. However, don't feel you must be *born* with discipline in order to have it. Discipline can be developed, though it won't happen overnight. You must want to succeed strongly enough that you'll do whatever it takes to change your lifestyle habits.

Now is the time to construct a basic financial plan for yourself. The reason I call this section a "basic" plan is because it may not take into account *all* of your financial needs and concerns. However, it's a great first step, especially for those of you who have done little planning before. As you become more knowledgeable with time, you will be able to build on what you do here. As basic as these exercises may appear, in doing them you will have done more for your financial future than nine out of ten Americans.

STEP 1: DETERMINE YOUR NET WORTH

You may have already completed the net worth statement located in Chapter 12, on estate planning. If you have, then you may refer to that statement. If not, or if you would simply like to do it again, please complete the statement shown below. The purpose of the net worth statement is to give you an idea of your financial status in real numbers, so that you may better determine where to go from there.

NET WORTH STATEMENT

Assets	Current Value
1. Liquid assets	_____
Checking accounts	500
Savings accounts	_____
Certificates of deposit	_____
Money market accounts	_____
Treasury Notes	_____
Cash on hand	_____
Other	_____
2. Negotiable securities (non-retirement)	_____
Stocks	_____
Bonds	_____
Mutual funds	_____
Other	_____
3. Retirement plans	
Company-sponsored	_____
IRAs	_____
Annuities	_____
4. Life insurance	_____
Cash value	_____
5. Real Estate	_____
Residence	_____
Other home	_____
Rental property	_____

6. Personal property

Antiques	50,00
Furnishings	50,00
Appliances	150
Autos	500
Boats	
Other vehicles	100
Computers	
Clothing	300
Jewelry	200
Tools	400
TVs, VCRs, etc. Radio	100
Other	900

Total Assets $ 2750

Liabilities

1. Mortage loans
   Primary residence
   Other homes
   Rental property

2. Installment loans

Automobiles	2300
Furniture	
Appliances	
Other	55000, 600

3. Miscellaneous loans
   Unsecured (credit cards)
   Other

Total Liabilities $ 57900

2750	–	57900	=	$ -55150
Total Assets		Total Liabilities		Current Net Worth

STEP 2: DETERMINE YOUR GOALS

Here you want to write down any financial goals you may
have, from retiring with $2,000,000 to buying a yacht. Don't
give any regard to time or money constraints at this point;
simply write down whatever you wish. You may want to relo-
cate to some place more conducive to thinking before you
start: by the pool, in a field, out in the woods, in the library.

1. Schooling at weimar
2. mission work 5 years
3. School loans payed off withn 2 year
4. Property (Ranch, Farm)
5. Boat
6. Travel world
7. Retire c million dollars
8. Rear 2 offspring
9. Farmer
10. Have invesment goals
11. _____
12. _____
13. _____
14. _____
15. _____
16. _____
17. _____
18. _____
19. _____
20. _____

STEP 3: DEFINE YOUR GOALS

At this point you want to begin weeding out the goals which are totally unrealistic, and to attribute some parameters to those which remain. After thinking about them a bit, rewrite the goals from Step 2, and this time indicate what you estimate the cost of the goals to be, as well as how long you estimate it will take (or you would like it to take) for the goals to be realized.

	Goal	Cost	Years to Achieve
1.	Pay school loan	41000	2
2.	Weimar	8600	1 yr
3.	Farm	100,000	10 yrs
4.	children		
5.	Travel		
6.	investments		
7.			
8.			
9.			
10.			
11.			
12.			
13.			
14.			
15.			
16.			
17.			
18.			
19.			
20.			

STEP 4: COMPUTE YOUR GOALS

Through the use of a financial calculator you can determine, among many other things, how much money you have to deposit each month in an investment to reach your goals. You should be somewhat familiar with how this works already as a result of the discussions in the chapters on retirement planning and college investing. Refer back to those chapters, as well as to the instruction books which came with your calculator, if you need help on the precise handling of the instrument. Note: Use 12% per year, or 1% per month, as the assumed interest rate for your calculations if you plan to use mutual funds.

Goal	Present Value	Future Value	Number of Yr/Mo. to Reach	Assumed Interest Rate	Monthly Deposit
1.					
2.					
3.					
4.					
5.					
6.					
7.					
8.					

STEP 5: INITIATE A MUTUAL FUND ACTION PLAN

At the rear of this book in Appendix C, you will find a comprehensive list of no-load mutual fund families. For Step 5, contact any three of those families and request a comprehensive packet on their funds. Ask for both a non-IRA and an IRA application, just to be sure you're covered if you decide to invest. To help you in your selection, I have produced a brief list below of the no-load families which accept low minimum investments.

Founders Funds	1-800-525-2440
Twentieth Century Investors	1-800-345-2021
Invesco	1-800-525-8085
Berger Group	1-800-333-1001
Janus Funds	1-800-525-3713

REVIEW LIST

Fund Family Called	Date Called	Notes

STEP 6: REDUCE YOUR AUTO INSURANCE COST

You will want to carefully review your automobile coverage at some point to see if you have taken advantage of everything you can to keep the cost down. However, there are two things you can do immediately to realize a savings.

A. Check your policy to see if you're carrying a deductible of $100 or $250. If you are, raise it to $500. You should realize a savings of about 25% per year. If you are already carrying a $500 deductible, determine if you can raise it to $1000, thereby realizing an even greater savings.

B. Shop around. Don't underestimate the value of doing this when it comes to automobile insurance. Rates for the same person can vary by as much as $1000 among insurance companies, according to *Consumer Reports*.

USAA	1-800-531-8319
Erie Insurance Exchange	1-800-458-0811
Nationwide Mutual	Check your Local Yellow Pages
Geico	1-800-841-3000
Liberty Mutual	Check your Local Yellow Pages
Prudential Property and Casualty	1-800-368-8868

STEP 7: SHOP AROUND FOR INSURANCE

Life Insurance

You should know by now that term life insurance is a much better alternative than cash value/whole life insurance. You can feel free to call the James L. Paris Insurance Services to receive a free quote on lowest-cost term life insurance. Even if you already have a term policy, call to see if we can find something which is less expensive but still high-quality. If you have been reluctant to buy life insurance because all you thought existed is expensive whole life, definitely call. If you have dependents, they should not go unprotected. To call, simply dial:

1-800-LIFE-560

Health Insurance

If you or your spouse is able to insure the whole family through a company-sponsored group plan, then that will be your best bet. If you have no coverage at all, you definitely need to get some. A medical misfortune of only moderate size can drive an unprepared family into bankruptcy. Get a Major Medical policy. Even though Major Medical won't cover you for every little thing, it will cover most expenses if you have an accident or a serious illness. In order to keep this coverage affordable, carry a deductible of $1000. This may seem high (especially since this means that all checkups will be on you), but it is the best way to ensure that you have coverage without paying too much.

Complete the form below and return it to James L. Paris Insurance Services to receive a record of the best medical plans for you and your family.

INSURANCE ANALYSIS REQUEST FORM
MEDICAL INSURANCE

For Individual and Family Medical quotes (there is no extra charge for family quotes):

Complete the information for each person to be covered.

_____ _____ _____ _____
Insured's Name   *Date of Birth* *Sex* *Smoker?*

_____ _____ _____ _____
Spouse's Name   *Date of Birth* *Sex* *Smoker?*

_____ _____ _____
Number of   *State*   *Zip Code*
Children

_____ _____
Country   *Occupation*

Deductible Categories: $100____ $250____ $500 ____ $1000 ____
$2500 ____ $5000 ___

Please print the name and address where the report(s) should be sent.

Name _____

Address _____

City _____ State _____ Zip _____

Home Phone Number ( )_____

Work Phone Number ( )_____

Send completed form to: James L. Paris Insurance Services
2270 Spring Lake Road, #400
Dallas, TX 75234

Normally this analysis sells for $24.95, but it is available to you on a complimentary basis as a purchaser of this book. (Please enclose $3.95 for postage and handling.)

STEP 8: COMPARISON SHOP
YOUR CREDIT CARDS

As discussed in Chapter 4, now would be a good time for you to start looking for a low-interest-rate credit card. For a listing of the best credit cards available, send for the free newsletter offer at the end of this book. Each month in the newsletter I list the best low-interest-rate credit cards in America. Be tenacious: If for some reason you are turned down by the first lender you apply to, simply apply with another lender, since there are many to choose from. Remember to take a cash advance and use this money to pay off the balances you may have on other high-interest-rate credit cards. Also be sure to cut those cards up to avoid the temptation of using them again.

STEP 9: CONSTRUCT A RETIREMENT PLAN

If you don't have a company-sponsored retirement plan available to you at work, you need to set up an Individual Retirement Account. By the time you reach this step, you may have received the mutual fund information I asked you to request earlier. If you have, consider opening any account designated for your retirement as an IRA. This is easy to do, and you should have received an IRA application from each of the fund families you contacted. If you have no retirement plan in place already, start an IRA now. Even if you are already covered by a company-sponsored plan, you can still open your own IRA, though you might not be able to deduct the contribution (depending on your income).

STEP 10: DEVELOP AN ESTATE PLAN

If you don't have a will, get one. It's that simple. Reading the chapter on estate-planning should have made you realize the dire consequences which can result if you die without a will. Consult an estate-planning attorney, or develop a do-it-yourself will. To receive a do-it-yourself will kit from the James L. Paris Organization, call 1-800-877-2022. The cost of the kit is $19.95.

If you have determined that you need a living trust, also contact an estate planning attorney as soon as possible. If you choose not to go to a lawyer, then at least get a do-it-yourself living trust in place. You may order such a kit from the James L. Paris Organization by calling 1-800-877-2022. The cost of the kit is $19.95.

Additional resources are available through . . .

James L. Paris Insurance Services	800-LIFE-560
James L. Paris Securities	800-950-PLAN
James L. Paris Financial Services	800-950-PLAN
James L. Paris Products	800-PARIS-92

CREDIT CARD SOURCES

The following list of unsecured credit cards represents the bank sources which typically offer the more competitive rates to applicants. However, the competitiveness can change at any time.

Unsecured Credit Cards

Amalgamated Bank
Chicago, IL
(312) 822-3000

AFBA Industrial Bank
Colorado Springs, CO
(800) 726-5075

Arkansas Federal
Little Rock, AR
(800) 477-3348

Central Carolina Bank
Durham, NC
(800) 577-1680

Citibank Choice
Towson, MD
(800) 462-4642

Consumer's Best/Signet
Richmond, VA
(800) 352-9995

Crestar Bank
Richmond, VA
(800) 368-7700

Federal Savings Bank
Rogers, AR
(800) 285-9090

Simmons Bank
Pine Bluff, AR
(501) 541-1000

Wachovia Bank
Atlanta, GA
(800) 241-7990

Secured Credit Cards

American Pacific Bank
Portland, OR
(800) 879-8745

Dreyfus Thrift
Old Beth Page, NY
(800) 727-3348

Community Bank of Parker
Parker, CO
(800) 779-8472

First Consumers
Seattle, WA
(800) 876-3262

SAMPLE CREDIT REPAIR LETTERS

**Sample Letter to Dispute an Inaccurate
Item on Your Credit Report**

Date

Your Name
Street Address
City, State, Zip

Name of Credit Bureau
Street Address
City, State, Zip

To: Customer Service

I have recently received a copy of my credit report as maintained by
your reporting agency. The copy I received contains information
which is inaccurate. As this information is both inaccurate and negative in nature, I am writing to request that it be investigated. The specific items I wish to have investigated are as follows:

> List the name of the creditor here.
> List the creditor code here.
> List the account number here.
> Describe inaccuracy here.

In accordance with the Fair Credit Reporting Act, I expect to be apprised of the results of this investigation within a reasonable period of time (30 days). I understand that the information is to be removed if it cannot be verified. If it is verified, I would like for you to forward to me the name and business address of the individual(s) with whom you verified the data, also per the Fair Credit Reporting Act. Once your investigation is complete, please send me an updated copy of my report.

Thank you for your consideration.

Sincerely,

Your signature here.
Your typed name here.
Your Social Security number here.
Your date of birth here.

Sample Letter to Dispute an Item on Your Credit Report Which Is Accurate But Negative

Date

Your Name
Street Address
City, State, Zip

Name of Credit Bureau
Street Address
City, State, Zip

To: Customer Service

I have recently received a copy of my credit report as maintained by your reporting agency. The copy I received contains the following information which I would like to have reverified immediately:

*   List the name of the creditor here.
      List the creditor code here.
      List the account number here.
      Describe inaccuracy here.

In accordance with the Fair Credit Reporting Act, I expect to be apprised of the results of this investigation within a reasonable period of time (30 days). I understand that the information is to be removed if it cannot be verified. If it is verified, I would like for you to forward to me the name and business address of the individual(s) with whom you verified the data, also per the Fair Credit Reporting Act. Once your investigation is complete, please send me an updated copy of my report.

Thank you for your consideration.

Sincerely,

Your signature here.
Your typed name here.
Your Social Security number here.
Your date of birth here.

Sample Letter to Request Removal of Information Which Is More Than Seven Years Old (Ten Years for a Bankruptcy)

Date

Your Name
Street Address
City, State, Zip

Name of Credit Bureau
Street Address
City, State, Zip

To: Customer Service

I have recently received a copy of my credit report as maintained by your reporting agency. The copy I received contains information which is over seven years old. Per the Fair Credit Reporting Act, I understand that you are responsible for deleting this information from my record. Please delete the following:

> List the name of the creditor here.
> List the creditor code here.
> List the account number here.

Once your investigation is complete, please send me an updated copy of my report.

Thank you for your consideration.

Sincerely,

Your signature here.
Your typed name here.
Your Social Security number here.
Your date of birth here.

Sample Letter to Follow Up a Request for a Reporting Agency Investigation from Which You Have Received No Response Within a Reasonable Period of Time

Date

Your Name
Street Address
City, State, Zip

Name of Credit Bureau
Street Address
City, State, Zip

To: Customer Service

On (date), I mailed a certified letter to your reporting agency which contained a request to have item(s) in my credit report investigated. Please find enclosed a copy of that original letter.

Thus far I have received no response. Per the Fair Credit Reporting Act, I am entitled to the results of that investigation within a reasonable period of time (30 days). Please forward the results of this investigation to me immediately, along with a copy of my updated credit report.

Thank you, once again, for your consideration.

Sincerely,

Your signature here.
Your typed name here.
Your Social Security number here.
Your date of birth here.

Sample Letter to Request Deletion of Unauthorized Credit Inquiries

Date

Your Name
Street Address
City, State, Zip

Name of Credit Bureau
Street Address
City, State, Zip

To: Customer Service

I have recently received a copy of my credit report as maintained by your reporting agency. The copy I received contains credit inquiries which I never authorized. I request that the following inquiries be immediately deleted:

> List the name of the creditor here.
> List the creditor code here.
> List the inquiry date here.

Once you have made the appropriate deletions, please send me an updated copy of my report.

Thank you for your consideration.

Sincerely,

Your signature here.
Your typed name here.
Your Social Security number here.
Your date of birth here.

NO-LOAD MUTUAL FUND FAMILY SOURCE DIRECTORY

AARP
P.O. Box 2540
Boston, MA 02208
(800) 253-2277

ACORN
227 West Monroe
Chicago, IL 60606
(800) 922-6769

AETNA
151 Farmington Avenue
Hartford, CT 06156
(800) 367-7732

AMERICAN HERITAGE
31 W. 52nd Street
New York, NY 10019
(212) 474-7308

AMERICAN PENSION
  INVESTORS
P.O. Box 2529
2303 Yorktown Avenue
Lynchburg, VA 24501
(800) 544-6060

ANALYTIC OPTIONED
  EQUITY
2222 Martin Street, Suite 230
Irvine, CA 92715
(800) 374-2633

BABSON
Three Crown Center
2440 Pershing Road, #G-15
Kansas City, MO 64108
(800) 422-2766

BARSON ASSET
450 Park Avenue
New York, NY 10022
(800) 992-2766

BARTLETT
26 E. Fourth Street, Suite 400
Cincinnati, OH 45202
(800) 800-4612

BENHAM
1665 Charleston Road
Mountain View, CA 94043
(800) 321-8321

BERGER
210 University Boulevard, #900
Denver, CO 80206
(800) 333-1001

BERWYN
1189 Lancaster Avenue
Berwyn, PA 19312
(800) 824-2249

BOSTON COMPANY
One Boston Place
Boston, MA 02108
(800) 225-5267

BRANDYWINE
3908 Kennett Pike
Greenville, DE 19807
(302) 656-6200

BULL AND BEAR
11 Hanover Square
New York, NY 10005
(800) 847-4200

CAPSTONE
P.O. Box 3167
1100 Milam, Suite 3500
Houston, TX 77253
(800) 262-6631

CENTURY SHARES
One Liberty Square
Boston, MA 02109
(800) 321-1928

CGM
222 Berkley Street, 19th Floor
Boston, MA 02116
(800) 345-4048

COLUMBIA
1301 S.W. Fifth Avenue
P.O. Box 1350
Portland, OR 97207
(800) 547-1707

COREFUND
680 E. Swedesford Road
Wayne, PA 19087
(800) 355-2673

CRABBE HUSON
121 S.W. Morrison Street, Suite
   1425
Portland, OR 97204
(800) 541-9732

DODGE AND COX
One Sansome Street, 35th Floor
San Francisco, CA 94104
(800) 621-3979

DREYFUS
200 Park Avenue
New York, NY 10166
(800) 645-6561

ECLIPSE
P.O. Box 2196
Peachtree City, GA 30269
(800) 872-2710

EVERGREEN
2500 Westchester Avenue
Purchase, NY 10577
(800) 235-0064

FIDELITY
82 Devonshire Street
Boston, MA 02109
(800) 544-8888

FIRST EAGLE
45 Broadway, 27th Floor
New York, NY 10006
(800) 451-3623

FLEX
6000 Memorial Drive
P.O. Box 7177
Dublin, OH 43017
(800) 325-3539

FORTY-FOUR WALL STREET
26 Broadway, Suite 205
New York, NY 10004
(800) 543-2620

FOUNDERS
2930 E. Third Avenue
Denver, CO 80206
(800) 525-2440

FREMONT
50 Fremont Street, Suite 3600
San Francisco, CA 94105
(800) 548-4539

GABELLI
One Corporate Center
Rye, NY 10580
(800) 422-3554

GALAXY
440 Lincoln Street
Worcester, MA 01653
(800) 628-0414

GATEWAY
400 Techne Center Drive,
    Suite 220
Milford, OH 45150
(800) 354-6339

GINTEL
6 Greenwich Office Park
Greenwich, CT 06831
(800) 243-5808

GIT
1655 N. Fort Myer Drive
Arlington, VA 22209
(800) 336-3063

GRADISON MCDONALD
580 Walnut Street
Cincinnati, OH 45202
(800) 869-5999

GREENSPRING
2330 West Joppa Road,
    Suite 110
Lutherville, MD 21093
(800) 366-3863

HARBOR
One Sea Gate
Toledo, OH 43666
(800) 422-1050

HIGHMARK
1900 Dublin-Granville Road
Columbus, OH 43229
(800) 433-6884

IAI
3700 First Bank Place
P.O. Box 357
Minneapolis, MN 55440
(800) 945-3863

INVESCO
P.O. Box 173706
Denver, CO 80217
(800) 525-8085

JANUS
100 Fillmore Street, Suite 300
Denver, CO 80206
(800) 525-3713

KAUFMANN
17 Battery Place, Suite 2624
New York, NY 10004
(800) 237-0132

KLEINWORT BENSON
200 Park Avenue, 24th Floor
New York, NY 10166
(800) 237-4218

LEGG MASON
111 S. Calvert Street
Baltimore, MD 21203
(800) 822-5544

LEPERCQ-ISTEL
1675 Broadway, 16th Floor
New York, NY 10019
(800) 338-1579

LEXINGTON
Park 80 W. Plaza 2
P.O. Box 1515
Saddle Brook, NJ 07662
(800) 526-0056

LINDNER
7711 Carondelet Avenue
P.O. Box 11208
St. Louis, MO 63105
(315) 727-5305

LOOMIS SAYLES
One Financial Center
Boston, MA 02111
(800) 633-3330

MATHERS
100 Corporate N., Suite 201
Bannockburn, IL 60015
(800) 962-3863

MAXUS
28601 Chagrin Boulevard, Suite 500
Cleveland, OH 44122
(216) 292-3434

MERIDIAN
60 E. Sir Francis Drake Boulevard
Wood Island, Suite 306
Larkspur, CA 94939
(800) 446-6662

MERRIMAN
1200 Westlake Avenue, N.
Seattle, WA 98109
(800) 423-4893

MIM
4500 Rockside Road, Suite 440
Independence, OH 44131
(800) 233-1240

MONETTA
1776-A S. Naperville Road,
   Suite 207
Wheaton, IL 60187
(800) 666-3882

MONTGOMERY
600 Montgomery Street
San Francisco, CA 94111
(800) 428-1871

MSB
330 Madison Avenue
New York, NY 10017
(212) 551-1920

MUTUAL
51 John F. Kennedy Parkway
Short Hills, NJ 07078
(800) 448-3863

NEUBERGER AND BERMAN
605 Third Avenue, 2nd Floor
New York, NY 10158
(800) 877-9700

NEW CENTURY
20 William Street
Wellesley, MA 02181
(617) 239-0445

NICHOLAS
700 N. Water Street,
   Suite 1010
Milwaukee, WI 53202
(800) 227-5987

NORTHEAST INVESTORS
50 Congress Street
Boston, MA 02109
(800) 225-6704

OAKMARK
Two N. LaSalle Street
Chicago, IL 60602
(800) 476-9625

OBERWEIS
841 North Lake Street
Aurora, IL 60506
(800) 323-6166

PACIFICA
230 Park Avenue
New York, NY 10169
(800) 662-8417

PAX
224 State Street
Portsmouth, NH 03801
(800) 767-1729

PERMANENT
P.O. Box 5847
Austin, TX 78763
(800) 531-5142

PERRITT
680 N. Lake Shore Drive
2038 Tower Offices
Chicago, IL 60611
(800) 338-1579

PORTICO
207 E. Buffalo Street, Suite 400
Milwaukee, WI 53202
(800) 228-1024

PRIMARY
First Financial Centre
700 N. Water Street
Milwaukee, WI 53202
(800) 443-6544

PRUDENT SPECULATOR
P.O. Box 75231
Los Angeles, CA 90075
(800) 444-4778

REICH AND TANG
100 Park Avenue
New York, NY 10017
(212) 830-5225

REYNOLDS
Wood Island, 3rd Floor
80 E. Sir Francis Drake Boulevard
Larkspur, CA 94939
(800) 338-1579

RIGHTIME
Forst Pavilion, Suite 3000
Wyncote, PA 19095
(800) 242-1421

ROBERTSON STEPHENS
One Embarcadero Center,
    Suite 3100
San Francisco, CA 94111
(800) 766-3863

ROYCE
1414 Avenue of the Americas
New York, NY 10019
(800) 221-4268

RUSHMORE
4922 Fairmont Avenue
Bethesda, MD 20814
(800) 622-1386

SAFECO
P.O. Box 34890
Seattle, WA 98124
(800) 426-6730

SALOMON BROTHERS
7 World Trade Center,
    38th Floor
New York, NY 10048
(800) 725-6666

SBSF
45 Rockefeller Plaza
New York, NY 10111
(800) 422-7273

SCHAFER
645 5th Avenue, 7th Floor
New York, NY 10022
(800) 343-0481

SCHRODER
787 Seventh Avenue
New York, NY 10019
(800) 344-8332

SCHWAB
101 Montgomery Street
San Francisco, CA 94104
(800) 526-8600

SCUDDER
160 Federal Street
Boston, MA 02110
(800) 225-2470

SENTRY
1800 N. Point Drive
Stevens Point, WI 54481
(800) 533-7827

SHERMAN, DEAN
60601 N.W. Expressway,
    Suite 465
San Antonio, TX 78201
(210) 492-1488

SIT
4600 Norwest Center
Minneapolis, MN 55402
(800) 332-5580

SOUND SHORE
P.O. Box 1810
8 Sound Shore Drive
Greenwich, CT 06838
(800) 551-1980

STEINROE
P.O. Box 1143
Chicago, IL 60690
(800) 338-2550

STRATTON
610 W. Germantown Pike,
   Suite 361
Plymouth Meeting, PA 19462
(800) 634-5726

STRONG
P.O. Box 2936
Milwaukee, WI 53201
(800) 368-3863

SWRW
300 Main Street
Cincinnati, OH 45202
(513) 621-2875

T. ROWE PRICE
10090 Red Run Boulevard
Owings Mills, MD 21117
(800) 638-5660

TWENTIETH CENTURY
4500 Main Street
P.O. Box 419200
Kansas City, MO 64141
(800) 345-2021

USAA
USAA Building
San Antonio, TX 78288
(800) 531-8181

UNITED SERVICES
P.O. Box 659
San Antonio, TX 78293
(800) 873-8637

VALUE LINE
711 Third Avenue
New York, NY 10017
(800) 223-0818

VANGUARD
Vanguard Financial Center
P.O. Box 2600
Valley Forge, PA 19482
(800) 662-7447

VISTA
P.O. Box 419292
Kansas City, MO 64179
(800) 348-4782

WARBURG-PINCUS
466 Lexington Avenue,
   10th Floor
New York, NY 10017
(800) 888-6878

WAYNE HUMMER
300 S. Wacker Drive
Chicago, IL 60606
(800) 621-4477

WILLIAM BLAIR
135 S. La Salle Street
Chicago, IL 60603
(800) 742-7272

WPG
One New York Plaza, 30th Floor
New York, NY 10004
(800) 223-3332

WRIGHT INTERNATIONAL
1000 LaFayette Boulevard
Bridgeport, CT 06604
(800) 888-9471

PUBLIC ORGANIZATION
SOURCE DIRECTORY

The following list includes groups, trade associations, and government organizations which can assist you with everything from lodging complaints against unscrupulous businesses to simply accessing more information about the various fields and specialties they represent.

Business

ALLIANCE AGAINST FRAUD
  IN TELEMARKETING
c/o National Consumers League
815 15th Street, NW, Suite 928N
Washington, DC 20005
(202) 639-8140

COUNCIL OF BETTER
  BUSINESS BUREAUS
4200 Wilson Boulevard, Suite 800
Arlington, VA 22203
(703) 276-0100

FEDERAL TRADE
  COMMISSION
6th and Pennsylvania Avenue, NW
Washington, DC 20580
(202) 326-2222

U.S. SMALL BUSINESS
  ADMINISTRATION
409 Third Street, SW, Suite 6100
Washington, DC 20416
(202) 205-6720

INTERSTATE COMMERCE
  COMMISSION
12th Street and Constitution
  Avenue, NW
Washington, DC 20423
(202) 927-5500

U.S. DEPARTMENT OF
  COMMERCE
14th Street
Washington, DC 20230
(202) 377-2000

General Consumer Affairs

CONSUMER INFORMATION
CENTER
18 F. Street, NW, Room G-142
Washington, DC 20405
(202) 566-1794

CALL FOR ACTION
3400 Idaho Avenue, NW, Suite 101
Washington, DC 20016
(202) 537-0585

CONSUMER FEDERATION OF
AMERICA
1424 16th Street, NW, Suite 604
Washington, DC 20036
(202) 387-6121

CONSUMER PRODUCT
SAFETY COMMISSION
5401 Westbard Avenue
Bethesda, MD 20207
(201) 492-6580

NATIONAL ASSOCIATION OF
CONSUMER AGENCY
ADMINISTRATORS
1010 Vermont Avenue, NW,
Suite 514
Washington, DC 20005
(202) 347-7395

NATIONAL CONSUMER
FRAUD TASK FORCE
1500 W. 23rd Street
Sunset Island, No. 3
Miami Beach, FL 33140
(305) 532-2607

OFFICE OF CONSUMER
AFFAIRS
U.S. Department of Commerce
14th and Constitution Avenue,
NW, Room H5718
Washington, DC 20230
(202) 482-5001

Dispute Resolution

AMERICAN ARBITRATION
ASSOCIATION
140 W. 51st Street
New York, NY 10020
(212) 484-1400

NATIONAL INSTITUTE FOR
DISPUTE RESOLUTION
1901 L. Street, NW, Suite 600
Washington, DC 20036
(202) 446-4764

Elderly Affairs

AMERICAN ASSOCIATION
OF RETIRED PERSONS
601 E. Street, NW
Washington, DC 20049
(202) 434-2277

ALZHEIMER'S DISEASE
EDUCATION AND
REFERRAL CENTER
P.O. Box 8250
Silver Spring, MD 20907
(800) 438-4380

ADMINISTRATION ON
  AGING
1112 16th Street, NW, Suite 100
Washington, DC 20036
(800) 677-1116

NATIONAL CLEARINGHOUSE
  FOR PRIMARY CARE
  INFORMATION
8201 Greensboro Drive,
  Suite 600
McLean, VA 22102
(703) 821-8955

U.S. SOCIAL SECURITY
  ADMINISTRATION
6401 Security Boulevard
Baltimore, MD 21235
(410) 965-7700

Food Concerns
FOOD SAFETY AND
  INSPECTION SERVICE
U.S. Department of Agriculture
Washington, DC 20250
(800) 535-4555

FOOD LABELING EDUCA-
  TION INFORMATION
  CENTER
Food and Nutrition Information
  Center
National Agricultural Library,
  Room 304
1031 Baltimore Boulevard
Bethsville, MD 20705
(301) 504-5719

FOOD AND DRUG
  ADMINISTRATION
5600 Fishers Lane
Rockville, MD 20857
(301) 443-3170

Health Affairs
AMERICAN MEDICAL
  ASSOCIATION
515 State Street
Chicago, IL 60610
(312) 464-4818

HEALTH AND HUMAN
  SERVICES HOTLINE
P.O. Box 17303
Baltimore, MD 21203-7303
(800) 368-5779

NATIONAL COUNCIL
  AGAINST HEALTH FRAUD
P.O. Box 1276
Loma Linda, CA 92354
(714) 824-4690

NATIONAL CLEARINGHOUSE
  FOR ALCOHOL AND
  DRUG INFORMATION
P.O. Box 2345
Rockville, MD 20847
(800) 729-6686

NATIONAL MATERNAL
  AND CHILD HEALTH
  CLEARINGHOUSE
8201 Greensboro Drive, Suite 600
McLean, VA 22102
(703) 821-8955

NATIONAL INSTITUTE FOR
OCCUPATIONAL SAFETY
AND HEALTH
4676 Columbia Parkway
Cincinnati, OH 45226
(800) 356-4674

NATIONAL CANCER
INSTITUTE
9000 Rockville Pike
Bethesda, MD 20892
(800) 4-CANCER

OFFICE ON SMOKING AND
HEALTH
c/o Centers for Disease Control
4770 Buford Highway
Mail Stop K-50
Atlanta, GA 30341-3724
(404) 488-5705

U.S. DEPARTMENT OF
HEALTH AND HUMAN
SERVICES
6325 Security Boulevard
Baltimore, MD 21207

Insurance Affairs
AMERICAN INSURANCE
ASSOCIATION
(Property and Casualty Only)
1130 Connecticut Avenue, NW,
Suite 1000
Washington, DC 20036
(202) 828-7100

NATIONAL INSURANCE CON-
SUMER ORGANIZATION
121 N. Payne Street
Alexandria, VA 22314
(307) 549-8050

WEISS RESEARCH, INC.
P.O. Box 2923
West Palm Beach, FL 33402
(407) 684-8100

Investment Affairs
COMMODITY FUTURES
TRADING COMMISSION
2033 K. Street, NW
Washington, DC 20581
(202) 254-6387

NATIONAL ASSOCIATION OF
SECURITIES DEALERS
1735 K. Street, NW
Washington, DC 20006
(202) 728-8000

SECURITIES AND EXCHANGE
COMMISSION
450 Fifth Street, NW
Washington, DC 20549
(202) 272-7440

Affairs of Law and Justice
AMERICAN BAR
ASSOCIATION
1800 M. Street, NW, Suite 200
Washington, DC 20036
(202) 331-2258

FEDERAL BUREAU OF
INVESTIGATION
United States Department of
Justice
10th Street and Pennsylvania
Avenue, NW
Washington, DC 20535
(202) 324-3000

NATIONAL INSTITUTE OF
JUSTICE
Box 6000, Dept. AID
Rockville, MD 20850
(800) 851-3420

OFFICE OF JUVENILE JUS-
TICE AND DELINQUENCY
PREVENTION
P.O. Box 6000
Rockville, MD 20850
(800) 638-8736

Real Estate Affairs
NATIONAL ASSOCIATION OF
HOME BUILDERS
15th and M Streets, NW
Washington, DC 20005
(202) 822-0200

NATIONAL ASSOCIATION OF
REALTORS
430 Michigan Avenue
Chicago, IL 60611-4087
(312) 329-8200

Tax Affairs
INTERNAL REVENUE
SERVICE
111 Constitution Avenue, NW
Washington, DC 20224
(202) 622-5000

Miscellaneous
AMERICAN SOCIETY OF
TRAVEL AGENTS
1101 King Street
Alexandria, VA 22314
(703) 739-2782

BANKCARD HOLDERS OF
AMERICA
560 Herndon Parkway, Suite 120
Herndon, VA 22070
(703) 481-1110

DEPARTMENT OF HOUSING
AND URBAN
DEVELOPMENT
451 7th Street, SW
Washington, DC 20410
(202) 708-0980

FEDERAL AVIATION
ADMINISTRATION
Public Inquiry
U.S. Department of
Transportation
Washington, DC 20591
(202) 267-3476

FEDERAL COMMUNICA-
TIONS COMMISSION
1919 M. Street, NW
Washington, DC 20554
(202) 632-7000

FEDERAL HIGHWAY
ADMINISTRATION
Office of Highway Safety
400 7th Street, SW
Washington, DC 20590

FEDERAL JOB INFORMATION
CENTER HOTLINE
(202) 606-2700

FEDERAL RESERVE SYSTEM
20th Street and Constitution
Avenue, NW
Washington, DC 20551
(202) 452-3244

INDOOR AIR QUALITY
INFORMATION
CLEARINGHOUSE
P.O. Box 37133
Washington, DC 20013-7133
(800) 438-4318

IMMIGRATION AND NATU-
RALIZATION SERVICE
425 I Street, NW
Washington, DC 20536
(202) 514-4316

NATIONAL ASSOCIATION OF
JEWELRY APPRAISERS
P.O. Box 6558
Annapolis, MD 21401-0558
(301) 261-8270

NATIONAL CLEARING-
HOUSE ON LITERACY
EDUCATION
c/o Center for Applied Linguistics
1118 22nd Street, NW
Washington, DC 20037
(202) 429-9292

NATIONAL INFORMATION
CENTER FOR CHILDREN
AND YOUTH WITH
DISABILITIES
P.O. Box 1492
Washington, DC 20013
(800) 999-5599

NATIONAL CHARITIES
INFORMATION BUREAU
19 Union Square West, 6th Floor
New York, NY 10003-3395
(212) 929-6300

OFFICE OF POLICY AND
PLANNING
U.S. Department of Education
400 Maryland Avenue, SW
Washington, DC 20202
(202) 401-0590

PATENT AND TRADEMARK
OFFICE
2011 Crystal Drive
Arlington, VA 22202
(703) 305-8341

UNITED NATIONS INFORMA-
TION CENTRE
1889 F. Street, NW, Ground Floor
Washington, DC 20006
(202) 289-8670

U.S. FISH AND WILDLIFE
SERVICE
1849 C. Street, NW
Washington, DC 20240
(703) 358-1724

U.S. ENVIRONMENTAL
PROTECTION AGENCY
401 M. Street, SW
Washington, DC 20460
(202) 260-7751

U.S. DEPARTMENT OF
VETERANS AFFAIRS
810 Vermont Avenue, NW
Washington, DC 20420
(800) 827-1000

U.S. DEPARTMENT OF THE
INTERIOR
18th and C Streets, NW
Washington, DC 20240
(202) 208-4871

UNITED STATES INFORMA-
TION AGENCY
301 Fourth Street, SW,
Room 602
Washington, DC 20547
(202) 619-4355

U.S. GEOLOGICAL SURVEY
P.O. Box 25286
Denver, CO 80225

U.S. CUSTOMS SERVICE
P.O. Box 7407
Washington, DC 20044
(202) 927-6724

U.S. DEPARTMENT OF STATE
Washington, DC 20520
(202) 647-6575

U.S. DEPARTMENT OF
LABOR
200 Constitution Avenue, NW,
Room N5666
Washington, DC 20210
(202) 219-8921

U.S. COPYRIGHT OFFICE
Library of Congress
Washington, DC 20559
(202) 707-3000

U.S. CUSTOMS SERVICE
1301 Constitution Avenue, NW
Washington, DC 20229
(202) 927-2095

U.S. POSTAL SERVICE
475 L'Enfant Plaza, SW
Washington, DC 20260-0010
(202) 268-2000

State Attorneys General

The role of the Attorney General is to serve as the chief law enforcement official within a given state. Many of the state consumer protection agencies in existence are actually subdivisions of the offices of attorneys general.

ALABAMA
Attorney General
11 South Union Street
Montgomery, AL 36130
(205) 242-7300

ALASKA
Attorney General
Department of Law
120 4th Street
Juneau, AK 99801
(907) 465-3600

ARIZONA
Attorney General
1275 West Washington
Phoenix, AZ 85007
(602) 542-4266

ARKANSAS
Attorney General
Office of the Attorney General
323 Center, Suite 200
Little Rock, AR 72201
(501) 682-2007

CALIFORNIA
Attorney General
Office of the Attorney General
Department of Justice
1515 K. Street, Law Library
Sacramento, CA 95814
(916) 324-5437

COLORADO
Attorney General
Department of Law
110 16th Street, 10th Floor
Denver, CO 80202
(303) 866-4500

CONNECTICUT
Attorney General
55 Elm Street
Hartford, CT 06106
(203) 566-2026

DELAWARE
Attorney General
Carvel State Office Building
820 North French Street
Wilmington, DE 19801
(202) 577-2500

FLORIDA
Attorney General
Department of Legal Affairs
The Capitol
Tallahassee, FL 32399
(904) 487-1963

GEORGIA
Attorney General
State Law Department
132 State Judicial Building
Atlanta, GA 30334
(404) 656-4585

HAWAII
Attorney General
Department of the Attorney
    General
425 Queen Street
Honolulu, HI 96813
(808) 586-1500

IDAHO
Attorney General
Office of the Attorney General
State Capitol
Boise, ID 83720
(208) 334-2424

ILLINOIS
Attorney General
500 South Second Street
Springfield, IL 62706
(217) 782-1090

INDIANA
Attorney General
219 State House
Indianapolis, IN 46204
(317) 232-6201

IOWA
Attorney General
Hoover State Office Building
Des Moines, IA 50319
(515) 281-5164

KANSAS
Attorney General
301 West Tenth, Judicial
    Center
Topeka, IA 66612
(913) 296-2215

KENTUCKY
Attorney General
State Capitol, Room 116
Frankfort, KY 40601
(502) 564-7600

LOUISIANA
Attorney General
Department of Justice
P.O. Box 94005
Baton Rouge, LA 70804
(504) 342-7013

MAINE
Attorney General
Department of Attorney
    General
State House Station #6
Augusta, ME 04333
(207) 626-8800

MARYLAND
Attorney General
200 Saint Paul Place
Baltimore, MD 21202
(410) 576-6550

MASSACHUSETTS
Attorney General
1 Ashburton Place
Boston, MA 02108
(617) 727-3688

MICHIGAN
Attorney General
525 West Ottawa
Law Building
Lansing, MI 48913
(517) 373-1110

MINNESOTA
Attorney General
102 State Capitol
St. Paul, MN 55155
(612) 297-4272

MISSISSIPPI
Attorney General
P.O. Box 220
Jackson, MS 39205
(601) 359-3680

MISSOURI
Attorney General
Supreme Court Building
P.O. Box 899
Jefferson City, MO 65102
(314) 751-3321

MONTANA
Attorney General
Department of Justice
215 North Sanders Street
Helena, MT 59620
(406) 444-2026

NEBRASKA
Attorney General
State Capitol, Room 2115
P.O. Box 94906
Lincoln, NE 68509
(402) 471-2682

NEVADA
Attorney General
Heroes Memorial Building
Capitol Complex
Carson City, NV 89710
(702) 687-4170

NEW HAMPSHIRE
Attorney General
State House Annex, Room 208
25 Capitol Street
Concord, NH 03301
(603) 271-3658

NEW JERSEY
Attorney General
Office of the Attorney General
Department of Law and Public
    Safety
Hughes Justice Complex,
    CN 081
Trenton, NJ 08625
(609) 292-8740

NEW MEXICO
Attorney General
Bataan Memorial Building
P.O. Box 1508
Santa Fe, NM 87501
(505) 827-6000

NEW YORK
Attorney General
Department of Law
State Capitol
Albany, NY 12224
(518) 474-7330

NORTH CAROLINA
Attorney General
Department of Justice
2 East Morgan Street
Raleigh, NC 27601
(919) 733-3377

NORTH DAKOTA
Attorney General
State Capitol, 1st Floor
600 East Boulevard
Bismarck, ND 58505
(701) 328-2210

OHIO
Attorney General
30 East Broad Street, 17th Floor
Columbus, OH 43266
(614) 466-3376

OKLAHOMA
Attorney General
112 State Capitol
Oklahoma City, OK 73105
(405) 521-3921

OREGON
Attorney General
Department of Justice
100 State Office Building
Salem, OR 97310
(503) 378-6002

PENNSYLVANIA
Attorney General
Strawberry Square, 16th Floor
Harrisburg, PA 17120
(717) 787-3391

RHODE ISLAND
Attorney General
72 Pine Street
Providence, RI 02903
(401) 274-4400

SOUTH CAROLINA
Attorney General
Dennis Building
P.O. Box 11549
Columbia, SC 29211
(803) 734-3970

SOUTH DAKOTA
Attorney General
State Capitol, 1st Floor
Pierre, SD 57501
(605) 773-3215

TENNESSEE
Attorney General
450 James Robertson Parkway
Nashville, TN 37243
(615) 741-6474

TEXAS
Attorney General
Capitol Station
P.O. Box 12548
Austin, TX 78711
(512) 463-2100

UTAH
Attorney General
236 State Capitol
Salt Lake City, UT 84114
(801) 538-1326

VERMONT
Attorney General
Pavilion Office Building
109 State Street
Montpelier, VT 05602
(802) 828-3171

VIRGINIA
Attorney General
Office of the Attorney General
101 North Eighth Street,
    5th Floor
Richmond, VA 23219
(804) 786-2071

WASHINGTON
Attorney General
Highway Licenses Building
M/S: PB-71
Olympia, WA 98504
(206) 753-6200

WEST VIRGINIA
Attorney General
Building 1, Room E-26
State Capitol Complex
Charleston, WV 25305
(304) 558-2021

WISCONSIN
Attorney General
Department of Justice
114 East State Capitol
P.O. Box 7857
Madison, WI 53707
(608) 266-1221

WYOMING
Attorney General
State Capitol
Cheyenne, WY 82002
(307) 777-7810

DISTRICT OF COLUMBIA
Corporation Counsel
Office of the Corporation
    Counsel
1350 Pennsylvania, NW,
    Room 329
Washington, DC 20004
(202) 727-6248

PUERTO RICO
Secretary
Department of Justice
P.O. Box 192
San Juan, PR 00904
(809) 721-2924

BIBLIOGRAPHY

Cassidy, Daniel J. *The Scholarship Book*. Englewood Cliffs, NJ: Prentice Hall, 1993.

Delgado, Raul A. *Car Buying and Leasing Exposed*. Costa Mesa, CA: Brianico, 1993.

Detweiler, Gerri. *The Ultimate Credit Handbook*. New York: Plume, 1993.

Dolan, Ken and Daria Dolan. *Smart Money*. New York: Berkley Publishing Group, 1990.

Easley, Bruce. *Biz-Op*. Port Townsend, WA: Loompanies Unlimited, 1994.

Jacobs, Sheldon. *The Handbook for No-Load Fund Investors*. Irvington-on-Hudson, NY: The No-Load Fund Investor, Inc., 1994.

Kraemer, Sandy F. *60 Minute Estate Planner*. Englewood Cliffs, NJ: Prentice Hall, 1994.

Lesko, Matthew. *Lesko's Info-Power*. Kensington, MD: Info, USA, 1990.

Polto, Pearl. *Pearl Polto's Easy Guide to Good Credit*. New York: Berkley Publishing Group, 1990.

Ross, James R. *How to Buy a Car*. New York: St. Martin's Press, 1992.

NOTES

1. Gerri Detweiler, *The Ultimate Credit Handbook* (New York: Plume, 1993), chapter 9.

2. See Gerri Detweiler, *The Ultimate Credit Handbook;* and Jordan E. Goodman and Sonny Bloch, *Everyone's Money Book* (Chicago: Dearborn Press, 1994), 399.